MW01493463

God, Me, & a Cup of Tea
Volume 3

101 devotional readings to savor
during your time with God

Michele Huey

God, Me & a Cup of Tea, Vol. 3:
101 devotional readings to savor during your time with God

Michele Huey
121 Homestead Lane
Glen Campbell, PA 15742
www.michelehuey. com

First Edition

ISBN- 9781694127853

Cover design by Lynnette Bonner of Indie Cover Design

Printed in the United States of America

To Sharon

Let the word of Christ dwell in you richly ...

–Colossians 3:16 KJV

Contents

The ABC's of Knowing God Better

Now this is eternal life:
that they know you, the only true God,
and Jesus Christ, whom you have sent.

–John 17:3 NIV

A: Alpha
Who's in Charge?

In the beginning God .... – Genesis 1:1 NIV

I am the Alpha and the Omega ... – Revelation 1:8; 21:6; 22:13 NIV

"GOD IS NOT OUR buddy or our errand boy," Marlene Bagnull notes in *Write His Answer,* her Bible study for Christian writers.

I read those words in 1996 and never forgot them. They extend into every area of my life, not just my writing and speaking.

You see, too often I forget who's in charge and treat God like my chum or my gopher (you know, go-fer-this, go-fer-that). I shoot up prayer requests like orders, expecting Him to answer when I want, which is usually right now, and the way I want. It's like I'm the master and He's the servant.

Yes, the Bible tells us to pray, to lay our requests before Him, to ask, to seek, to knock, the cast all our cares on Him, and He will hear and will answer. In fact, He knows our needs before we even ask.

But none of the verses I've alluded to tell us to tell Him how to answer or when to answer.

In our me-first world, we tend to think we're in charge.

Mankind has always had that problem—thinking he's the center of the universe. Remember the uproar when Copernicus, in the sixteenth century, theorized that the earth revolved around the sun? How dare him! It wasn't until the next century that Galileo and his telescope proved him right.

But we still have that problem of putting ourselves as the center of the universe. Everything and everyone else, including God, revolves around us and our wants. Just look at the way people drive. Me-first. Get out of my way. The rules of the road aren't for me, so why should I use turn signals, stop at stop signs (isn't slowing down enough?), or turn on my headlights when it's raining or dusky? And if you're going too slow for me, I'll ride your tail until you speed up or I get a chance to pass you, even in a no-passing zone.

Yikes!

The Bible begins with four simple words: *In the beginning God.*

In the beginning of what? Of the created universe. Of time.

In the beginning God was already there. He created time.

The Hebrew word used for God in Genesis 1:1 is *Elohim*, and means "mighty God or supreme God." Another name for God is *Adonai*, translated "Lord" and means "Master or owner of all things." And why wouldn't He be? He created it all.

God is the Alpha (the first letter of the Greek alphabet), and everyone knows the Alpha is the undisputed leader of the pack.

God is the Omega (the last letter of the Greek alphabet), the One who remains standing after the final battle is fought, after the earth as we know it disappears, after a new heaven and a new earth appear, after time ends and eternity begins.

God is creator, master, the sovereign Lord of all that happens from the beginning to the end, the One who rules over human history.

He's not anybody's good buddy or errand boy.

Remind me, Lord, that You, not I, are the One in charge. You are Adonai, the Alpha of my life. Amen.

MORE TEA: Read and reflect on Genesis 1; Revelation 21–22.

B: Bread of Life

I have treasured the words of His mouth more than my daily bread. – Job 23:12 NIV

"I am the bread of life. He who comes to Me will never go hungry." – Jesus, as quoted in John 6:35 NIV

MY LATE FATHER-IN-LAW used to say a meal wasn't complete without bread.

I, myself, have always loved bread—fresh out of the oven, toasted, stuffed with potatoes and cheese, smeared with spicy tomato sauce and piled high with cheese and pepperoni and, occasionally a variety of vegetables, such as black olives and green peppers.

Bread has been a staple since man first figured out what to do with wheat. It has been called "the staff of life," the mainstay of man's diet.

Bread is mentioned all through the Bible: from Abraham serving bread to three heavenly visitors to his descendants strapping on their kneading bowls at the start of the exodus from Egypt; from God providing bread from heaven (manna) while they trekked the wilderness to the Promised Land to feeding bread baked on a hot stone to the depressed prophet Elijah centuries later as he fled the murderous Jezebel; from Jesus multiplying a few loaves to feed a crowd that numbered in the thousands to Him breaking bread at the last supper and telling His disciples, "This is My body, broken for you" and then breaking bread after accompanying two dejected, puzzled disciples to Emmaus after His resurrection. Bread is mentioned as early as Genesis 3:19.

Bread provides our bodies with needed fiber and vitamin B, which is essential to our digestive system and helps our bodies to use energy.

So why does bread get such a bad rap these days?

A loaf of bread made today with refined, enriched flour and loaded with preservatives to give it a longer shelf life is nothing like the bread our ancestors ate. We've so filled our stomachs with non-nutritional carbohydrates that adding bread to our daily diet overloads our systems. Low-carb diets, in which bread is a forbidden food, abound.

And so what was once the staff of life becomes a banned substance because we've developed cravings for sugars and starches that add the pounds.

And because we've become such a sedentary society. In biblical times, most people walked wherever they wanted to go. They worked in the fields, raising crops or animals. They lived physically demanding lives. No motorized wheels to help them get around (or wheels on the bottom of desk chairs).

"Why spend money on what is not bread, and your labor on what does not satisfy?" God admonishes us through the prophet

Isaiah. "Listen, listen to me, and eat what is good, and your soul will delight in the richest of fare" (Isaiah 55:2).

The richest of fare: God Himself.

Jesus said He is the Bread of Life. He provides us with what we need to live healthy spiritual lives, now and for all eternity.

His Word is bread to the spiritually hungry.

"Man shall not live by bread alone, but by every word that proceeds from the mouth of God," Jesus told His tempter in Matthew 4:4, quoting the Old Testament (Deuteronomy 8:3).

God's Word is our daily bread.

Jesus is the Staff of Life.

Tell me, do you include Bread in your daily diet?

Make me hungry for You, O Lord. Amen.

MORE TEA: Read and reflect on John 6:25–59.

C: Compassionate God

When he cries out to me, I will hear, for I am compassionate. – Exodus 22:27 NIV

The LORD is compassionate and gracious, slow to anger and abounding in love. – Psalm 103:8 NIV

WHEN I WAS RESEARCHING historical background for Part 1 of my novel, *The Heart Remembers*, which is set in Vietnam during the war, I discovered an interesting fact: Medical teams from the military hospitals were often sent into nearby villages when there was a lull in their hectic schedules to treat the locals. One of the places they visited was the Quy Hoa Leper Hospital in Binh Dinh province.

I was intrigued not only by the compassion shown by U.S. troops in the middle of an ugly war but also by the way this hospital treated lepers.

The hospital itself is located in a secluded cove, surrounded by mountains on three sides, with one of the nicest beaches in the area as the fourth boundary. But far from being depressing, the hospital grounds are more like a resort, and the patients live with their families in small, well-kept houses. They work, too—

in the rice fields, the fishing industry, and in repair and craft shops.

That's a far cry from the way lepers were treated in biblical times, when they were the "untouchables," forbidden to associate with anyone else but another leper. They were to cry out "Unclean!" whenever healthy people were in the vicinity, and if someone touched a leper, that person was considered defiled and was then shunned.

Unable to live with their loved ones, lepers were relegated to colonies outside the town limits and, being unemployable, begged for handouts to survive.

We can understand the desperation the leper felt when he approached Jesus, dropped down on his knees, and said, "If you are willing, you can make me clean."

The Son of God did not shun him. Instead, "filled with compassion, Jesus reached out his hand and touched the man. 'I am willing,' he said."

I like the way The Message phrases it: "Deeply moved, Jesus put out his hand, touched him, and said, 'I want to. Be clean.'"

The Son of God didn't have to touch the leper. He *wanted* to. It would have been better if he hadn't. Now he'd be considered defiled. But as one commentary put it, "Jesus' compassion for the man superseded ceremonial considerations."

Compassion is defined as "sharing the hurts of another and wanting to help."

It's one thing to feel sorry for someone. But it's another to feel so sorry that you have to do something—anything—to help that person.

Think of the outpouring of love and help when disaster strikes: when Hurricane Sandy devastated the Eastern Seaboard, when a mentally unstable gunman shot and killed twenty children, ages six and seven, and six adults at Sandy Hook Elementary School. Or 9/11. People with no connections to anyone in the disaster-stricken areas dropped what they were doing, loaded up provisions, and drove hours to find a way to help.

Compassion trumps policy, procedure, ritual, ceremony, even common sense. Compassion is what drove Jesus. Compassion is what drives God. It is why he sent his Son to die in our place.

But we don't have to wait until disaster strikes to show compassion. We can show it every day. Just look around. Ask God to open your eyes.

Who are the lepers in your world? The untouchables? The ones outside the city gate, shunned by "decent folks"?

Who can you reach out and touch today?

Fill me with Your compassion, Lord! Amen.

MORE TEA:

Read and reflect on Lamentations 3:21–23, 32; Mark 1:40–45.

D: Deliverer God

The LORD is my rock, my fortress, and my deliverer. – Psalm 18:2 NIV

For He will deliver the needy when they cry out. – Psalm 72:12 NIV

I SHOULD HAVE KNOWN better than to even try.

But when Rachael called Wednesday and kindly chastised me for neglecting our Tuesday-Thursday exercise dates for the past month, I told her I'd see her the next day.

I figured by one o'clock the warmer temperatures and the rain would melt the mess in the driveway and the lane. So after a light lunch of yogurt and granola, I laced up my hiking boots, zipped up my Carhartt hoodie, stuffed my exercise sneakers in a plastic bag, and grabbed an umbrella.

I could have waited until it stopped pouring. I could have said "Nuts with it" when I saw the ice in the driveway. I could have driven my truck the two-tenths of a mile to Rachael's.

But I wanted to walk. The recent parade of snowstorms, frigid temperatures, and wind had intimidated this senior citizen to stay indoors. I missed being outside. When I bundled up and stepped out into the winter sunshine for a one-mile walk, I felt better for days.

There was no sunshine Thursday. Only overcast skies and, when I headed for Rachael's, a downpour. But I was determined to walk the short distance. I mean, how bad could it be?

Sometimes being stubborn isn't good.

I surveyed the rain-covered skating rink that was my driveway. Too risky. I headed for the yard, where the snow would give me traction. Not a good idea, considering the snow came to my knees. I tried stepping in the deer tracks, but still I landed on my tushie. If any of my neighbors had been watching, I'm sure they could have gotten a good submission to *America's Funniest Home Videos*.

Somehow I managed to get back on my feet and to the road, where I followed the bare spots. I made it to within a hundred feet of my destination then stopped. The rest of the way was a sheet of ice. I imagined myself sprawled on the glistening lane in the downpour, unable to get back up. Retreat was a risky option, as the road behind me was getting more slippery by the second, thanks to the rain.

Swallowing my pride, I pulled out my cell phone called Rachael, who backed up her SUV to where I stood and delivered me from my predicament.

Sometimes in life we get ourselves into jams and need someone to deliver us, but we're too proud to ask. So we slog on, getting ourselves in deeper and deeper.

There is no place in the Bible where it says, "God helps those who help themselves." On the contrary, God wants us to realize our need for Him (see Matthew 5:3). He's there for us all the time, any time we need Him, whether the need is great or small (see Psalm 55:17). He is our Deliverer.

If He sent His Son to deliver us from sin's eternal penalty, won't He surely deliver us from the sometimes silly predicaments into which we get ourselves?

Oh, He won't miraculously pluck us up from an icy roadway, but He can send someone to help, show us the way out, or give us the wisdom, courage, and strength we need follow His directions.

All we have to do is swallow our pride and ask.

Deliver me from myself, O Lord! Amen.

MORE TEA: Read and reflect on Psalm 107.

E: Eternal One

Abraham planted a tamarisk tree in Beersheba, and there he called on the name of the LORD, the Eternal One. – Genesis 21:33 NIV

He has also set eternity in the hearts of men. – Ecclesiastes 3:11b NIV

THERE'S A SCENE IN *Macbeth* in which Shakespeare, who wrote the play to get on the good side of King James I, uses an apparition of a line of eight kings, the last one holding a mirror, to imply that the family of James I would hold the throne forever.

Forever. Eternity. That's a long time. In fact, it isn't time. Because time is measured—in seconds, minutes, hours, days, weeks, months, years, decades, centuries, millennia. Eternity cannot be measured. There is no time as we know it in eternity.

The apostle Peter tried to explain it when he wrote, "With the Lord a day is like a thousand years, and a thousand years are like a day" (2 Peter 3:8).

We've come to the letter "E" in our series of getting to know God better using the letters of the alphabet.

God is *eternal.* His being spans past, present, and future. "I am the Alpha and the Omega," he says in Revelation, "the One who is, who was, and who is to come" (1:8).

God had no beginning. He always has been.

God *is*, present tense. Contrary to the belief of nineteenth century German philosopher Freidrich Nietzsche, which has echoed down through the centuries, God is not dead.

God will always be. A mirror facing a mirror into infinity.

What does this have to do with us?

For the answer, I turn to God's Word:

"He has placed eternity in the hearts of men" (Ecclesiastes 3:11).

"The LORD God formed man from the dust of the ground *and breathed into his nostrils the breath of life*, and man became a living being" (Genesis 2:7).

God Himself breathed life into us.

We are not just physical bodies walking around on the planet. We are also mental beings because we have a brain. We are emotional beings because we have a heart that feels joy and pain and everything in between. We are spiritual beings because we have a soul that God breathed into us, a spirit that is restless and empty until we anchor ourselves in the One who made us and Who calls to us to know Him, fill our empty selves with Himself, with His life, and spend eternity with Him.

"Lord, Thy madest us for Thyself," wrote St. Augustine, "and we can find no rest till we find rest in Thee."

"Since were made for eternity," one commentator notes, "the things of time cannot fully and permanently satisfy."

Jesus' words to the Samaritan woman whom He met at the well reverberate through time to us today: "Whoever drinks the water I give him will never thirst. Indeed, the water I give him will become in him a spring of water welling up into eternal life" (John 4:14).

"He has placed eternity in the hearts of men." God has placed in each of us a longing that cannot be satisfied with anything but Him.

"You will seek me and find me when you seek me with all your heart," God tells us (Jeremiah 29:13).

God is eternal, and He wants to share eternity with you.

Have you found Him? Are you seeking?

He isn't far—only a breath away.

Thank You, Father, that You loved me so much that You made the way for me to spend eternity with You. Amen.

MORE TEA: Read and reflect on 1 John 5:11–12.

F: Faithful God
Semper Fi

Thy steadfast love, O LORD, extends to the heavens, thy faithfulness to the clouds. – Psalm 36:5 RSV

If we are faithless [do not believe and are untrue to Him], He remains true (faithful to His Word and His righteous character), for He cannot deny Himself. – 2 Timothy 2:13 AMP

ONE OF MY FAVORITE shows when I was growing up was *The Lone Ranger*. I remember how Tonto often called him "Kimo sabe." I never knew what "Kimo sabe" meant until the named popped up while I was writing *The Heart Remembers*. Curious, I looked it up online.

"Kimo sabe," I learned, means "faithful friend."

How perfect, I thought. My novel is about love and faithfulness.

Faithfulness.

Someone who is faithful always does what he says he will do, no matter what. Someone who is faithful remains loyal in what she thinks, says and does.

The motto for the U.S. Marine Corps is *Semper Fidelis*—Always faithful. Faithful in all ways.

My husband is a former Marine. Semper Fi describes him perfectly. He is faithful, loyal and true to the core. I'm a blessed woman.

Twice blessed. Not only is my husband faithful, but my God is also.

Life can get pretty frightening at times, the future a big question mark. Things haven't panned out the way we'd planned. What next?

During the taping of a radio interview, WMUG radio personality Lillian O. Clemons once told me she leaves jigsaw puzzle pieces around everywhere—in the rooms of her house, in her car—to remind her when life doesn't make sense that she sees only a piece of the puzzle. God alone sees the entire picture.

"I love that analogy," I told her. "I can't see the future. I don't know what tomorrow holds. But when I look back on my life, I can see how God was working to prepare me for where I am now, what I'm facing today. I know I can trust God with my future because He's always had my back in the past."

Even when I didn't know Him, God knew me, had a plan and purpose for me (see Psalm 138:8; Psalm 139). When I thought I was the one in control, when I ignored God and went my own way, did my own thing, God gave me the freedom to wander.

A verse in a song I wrote describes this period of my life: "Now the path I chose was wide, all my hopes and dreams were there. I was having so much fun chasing rainbows in the air. But in time they disappeared, and all that remained were empty hopes and broken dreams and a heart full of pain."

That's when I came to Peniel (see the story of Jacob in Genesis 28 and 32), where faithful God was waiting for unfaithful me. That's where I wrestled, surrendered, and found forgiveness, hope, and unconditional love. That's where I experienced a true heart change. Where I realized "self control" was dangerous. What I needed for a fulfilled life was "God control."

"Never be afraid to trust an unknown future to a know God," Corrie ten Boom, author of *The Hiding Place*, once said.

I began trusting God with the next step. And the next one.

And I haven't ever, even for a second, regretted it.

Thank You, Father God, that You are faithful even when I'm not. Thank You for Your mercies that are new every morning. Amen.

MORE TEA: Read and reflect on Lamentations 3:22, 23.

G: God Is Good

Taste and see that the LORD is good. – Psalm 34:8 NIV

"I am the good shepherd." – Jesus, as quoted in John 10:11, 18 NIV

AS A CHILD, I was strongly encouraged to be good—obey my parents and teachers, respect my elders, do my homework, inform my parents of my whereabouts and call if I was going to be late. I wasn't to do anything that would bring shame and dishonor to the family name. My parents taught me that "a good name is more desirable than great riches" (Proverbs 22:1).

I attended a good school—one with a reputation for academics, discipline, and a faith-based curriculum. My parents were good people—honest, hardworking, faithful.

I was taught to believe that good will triumph over evil.

Foods may taste good but sometimes aren't good for your health. A relationship may be good or bad. Ideas may be good or bad, and sometimes we have to wait to find out. Actions are good or bad. Are there any in between? Declaring something "good" requires judgment, and aren't we supposed to not judge?

But some things are clearly good and some clearly bad. If you read Scripture, it isn't hard to figure out which is which.

God's Word sets the standard, draws a clear line between good and bad.

In the beginning, God declared all He created "good" (see Genesis 1). How could creation not reflect the Creator? And the Creator is good.

God didn't become good. He always was good. God cannot lose His goodness. He is, was, and always will be everything the word encompasses.

What does "good" encompass? My dictionary defines "good" as "excellent; right, as it ought to be; desirable; satisfying; pleasant; kind; friendly; real, genuine; beneficial." To that I add: "whatever is true, noble, right, pure, lovely, admirable, excellent, and praiseworthy" (Philippians 4:8).

I look at today's world and think we as a society have stopped believing in good. Life and culture have led us to believe that evil has eclipsed good. That good is weak, and bad is strong. That "good" is a thing of the past.

I refuse to believe that. Good is still a force to be reckoned with. Good is still stronger than evil.

How do I know?

Because God is good. And God is not dead. Nor is He passive. He's very much alive and active in the world today.

I chose today's Scripture readings, Psalm 23 and John 10, carefully. Meditate on all the Good Shepherd does for you personally: He leads, He provides, He protects, He restores, He refreshes, He comforts, He loves—so much that He laid down His own life so you, the sheep, may live.

"The LORD is good to all," the psalmist writes, "He has compassion on all that He has made" (Psalm 145:9). Still true.

"The earth is full of the goodness of the LORD" (Psalm 33:5 NKJV.

We need only eyes to see, ears to hear, and a heart that responds in childlike faith and trust. What you focus on is what you see.

It's your choice.

Open my eyes, my heart, my mind, and my spirit to Your goodness, O Lord. Amen.

MORE TEA: Read and reflect on Psalm 23; John 10:1–18.

H: Holy God

Holy, holy, holy is the LORD almighty. – Isaiah 6:3 NIV

"I am the LORD your God; consecrate yourselves and be holy, because I am holy." – Leviticus 11:44 NIV

But just as He who called you is holy, so be holy in all you do; for it is written, "Be holy, because I am holy." – 1 Peter 1:15–16 NIV

OF ALL GOD'S ATTRIBUTES, I struggle with His holiness the most. He is perfect, totally and completely pure. He cannot sin. It's not His nature. His Word says He cannot even look upon sin: "Your eyes are too pure to look on evil; You cannot tolerate wrong" or "look on wickedness" (Habakkuk 1:13).

While I don't consider myself evil or wicked, neither am I perfect. I feel much like Isaiah in today's reading: "Woe to me! I am ruined! For I am a man of unclean lips, and I live among a people of unclean lips, and my eyes have seen the King, the LORD Almighty."

Or the apostle Peter, when, courtesy of a Jesus miracle, returned with the catch of a lifetime: "Go away from me, Lord, for I am a sinful man" (Luke 5:8).

That's what understanding—truly understanding—God's holiness does to us. Instead of strutting around, complaining, defiantly declaring that God has some explaining to do when we get to heaven, we fall on our faces before Him, utterly undone because we finally understand His holiness and our unholiness.

But we are not undone.

"Then one of the seraphs flew to me with a live coal in his hand, which he had taken with tongs from the altar. With it he touched my mouth and said, 'See, this has touched your lips; your guilt is taken away and your sin atoned for'" (Isaiah 6:7).

And what did Jesus say to Peter? "Don't be afraid; from now on you will catch men" (Luke 5:10).

God is holy, yes. We, by nature, are unholy. But we don't have to clean up our act. God Himself washes us.

"As far as the east is from the west, so far has He removed our transgressions from us" (Psalm 103:12).

"Though your sins are like scarlet, they shall be white as snow" (Isaiah 1:18).

Sin carries with it the death sentence, but God has inked a pardon in his Son's blood: "For God so loved the world that He gave His only begotten Son, that whoever believes in Him should not perish but have everlasting life" (John 3:16). "The blood of His Son Jesus Christ cleanses us from all sin" (1 John 1:7)

In our stead, Jesus went to the death chamber—and came out alive three days later, releasing us from the power and punishment of sin. (Read Hebrews 9 and 10.)

I don't need to struggle with or be intimidated by holiness. Because, while God requires His children to be holy, He provides a way—the only way (see John 14:6)—for us to become holy and enter into His presence, now and forever.

Father, I feel so unworthy of the sacrifice Your Son made for me. Help me to live my life in such a way that Your implanted divine nature in me matures and produces a harvest for You. Amen.

MORE TEA: Read and reflect on Isaiah 6:1–9.

I: Immutable God

For I am the LORD, I do not change. –Malachi 3:6 NKJV

. . . like clothing they will be changed. But You are the same, and Your years will never end. – Hebrews 1:12 NRSV

EVERY THURSDAY ON FACEBOOK, it's "Throwback Thursday," when pictures of folks in years gone by are posted online. It's amazing to see the changes—in clothing and hairstyles, how much the kids have grown, how thin I was. TBT pictures never fail to get comments: "Look at those 80s glasses!" or "That dress is definitely 70s." "WOW! Time does move along very fast." Or (my personal favorite) "Wasn't that just yesterday?"

When I was young, I craved change. I didn't want to get old and set in my ways. I didn't want to be like my mother, who, I'd jokingly said, was like concrete—all mixed up and permanently set. I didn't want to be ready for bed Saturday evenings at nine. I wanted to be on my way to a night of dancing with my friends.

Well, guess what? I'm showered and in my jammies by eight and in bed by ten. Forty years brought a heap of changes. Some I like and some I don't.

Nothing in this world is permanent—not even concrete, which over time wears down and develops cracks. Our bodies grow old and wear out, no matter what we do to try to prevent or reverse the process. Time moves on, bringing changes to people, places, and things.

I think back to our years at "the Ridge," which we called the small country church we attended a few miles from our home in Smithport. I miss the people and the fun we had. I miss Paul and Sue, Steve and Jan, Sam and Deb, Pastor Bob and Edna, Carl and Louise, Mark and Chippie, a few of the many wonderful folks who made up our church family. We raised our kids together. We studied the Bible together. We picnicked and camped out together, planned VBS and holiday programs together. We shared many a carry-in supper.

But I couldn't go back and expect things to be the same. For one, Carl, Louise, and Edna are in heaven. Sam and Deb have moved from the area, as have Paul and Sue, who now are retired and live out-of-state. What I wouldn't give for one more picnic on the hill!

Yes, change is inevitable in this world.

But not in the next. Glory hallelujah! Because my next stop is heaven, God's home. Heaven will not change, except for new souls arriving, because God does not change.

That's why Jesus told us, "Do not lay up for yourselves treasures on earth, where moth and rust destroy and where thieves break in and steal; but lay up for yourselves treasures in heaven, where neither moth nor rust destroys and where thieves do not break in and steal. For where your treasure is, there your heart will be also" (Matthew 6:19–21 NKJV).

We'll deal with change for the rest of our lives. But, thank God, we can count on His unchanging grace—now and in eternity.

*"Swift to its close ebbs out life's little day; earth's joys grow dim, its glories pass away; change and decay in all around I see; O Lord who changes not, abide with me." * Amen.*

*From "Abide with Me" by Henry F. Lyte. In public domain.

MORE TEA:

Read and reflect on Hebrews 1:10–12; Numbers 23:19.

J: God Is Just
It Isn't Fair!

He is the Rock, His works are perfect, and all His ways are just. A faithful God who does no wrong, upright and just is He. – Deuteronomy 32:4 NIV

For the Son of Man is going to come in his Father's glory with his angels, and then He will reward each person according to what they have done. – Matthew 16:27 NIV

ONE MY SUMMER SESSION classes in college was a three-hour-long literature course, taught by a professor who stood behind the podium and read from his notes. Very little interaction with students. Fortunately we had a short break midway through the morning to give us some respite from the utter monotony.

I wasn't one to skip classes. The class notes were as important as out-of-class reading assignments when it came time to take his challenging essay exams, which we endured every Friday. I'd made the Dean's List each semester so far and had my eye on graduating at least *cum laude*.

During break time the professor also stepped out of the classroom, leaving his notes on the podium and his briefcase open on the desk. One Thursday when he left, a group of students huddled around the desk, one student rifling through the briefcase while another stood guard at the door.

"Here it is!"

While the rest of the class copied the essay questions for Friday's test, I sat glued to my seat, a sinking feeling growing in my stomach. The professor graded on a curve. What chance did I have of getting a good grade?

I studied hard anyway. Test day came. I knew when I handed in my paper my best wouldn't be enough. I went straight to the dorm and phoned home collect. Between sobs, I spilled out the story to my parents. Later that afternoon Dad showed up, having driven two hours to take me home for the weekend.

The following week we got our tests back. I received a C. The other students—the cheaters—had gotten A's.

It isn't fair! I thought, blinking back tears.

After class, I waited until the classroom emptied then approached the professor.

"I don't think this is a fair grade," I began, swallowing the lump in my throat. How could I tell him why? I wasn't a tattle-tale.

He shrugged, not even looking at me. "You just didn't do as well as the others."

"Thanks to you, you stupid jerk," I wanted to say. But I didn't. No sense in antagonizing the one who determined my final course grade. And sometimes professors could be, well, arbitrary.

I received (note I didn't write "earned') a C in the course, only the second throughout my entire college career. (The other was in philosophy, but I was happy just to pass that class.)

Sometimes we just have to take our lumps. Sometimes it seems as though unfairness rules the day. That those who do wrong prevail and those who do right suffer.

But I know my God is just and fair and in control. Someday we'll all receive recompense, reward for good, punishment for bad.

In the meantime, know that when we call to Him, crying, our heavenly Father will drop whatever He's doing to comfort, console, and counsel us.

And that's better than an A any day!

Thank You, Father, that whether it be morning, evening, or noon, when I cry out in distress, You hear my voice. (Psalm 55:17). Amen.

MORE TEA: Read and reflect on Psalm 37.

K: Kind God
Showing God's Kindness to Others

I have loved you with an everlasting love; I have drawn you with loving kindness. – Jeremiah 31:3 NIV

And now God can always point to us as examples of how very, very rich his kindness is, as shown in all he has done for us through Jesus Christ. – Ephesians 2:7 TLB

"LORD, WHEN I GET home, I could go for a bowl of homemade chicken soup!"

I'd just delivered my second baby by Caesarean section and was feeling weak, tired, and depressed. How I envied those women who had their babies naturally! They were up and about with a day. Not me. I'd be bedridden for a week in the hospital, then another week after I got home. I just didn't bounce back after childbirth like others did.

I longed for my mother's homemade chicken soup, which had always made me feel better. But Mom, a victim of Alzheimer's disease, was two hundred miles away and most of the time didn't even remember who I was.

How am I going to take care of a newborn baby and an active toddler? I wondered. My husband couldn't take any more time off work. When my first child was born, Mom spent a month with us, cleaning, washing, cooking, and making me chicken soup.

"I'll just have to do my best," I sighed, settling deeper beneath the blanket.

A week later I was home in bed when my friend, Sharon, walked in carrying a tray.

"I brought you some homemade chicken soup," she announced.

"How did you know I wanted homemade chicken soup? I never told anyone."

She put the tray on the nightstand. "The ladies in our Bible study group signed up to bring one meal a day to your family while you're still in bed this week. We figured supper would be the best time for you. Is that all right?"

I nodded, feeling awed that the God who runs the universe would actually answer a prayer for chicken soup.

That was forty years ago. Many times since I've experienced His loving kindness through someone's words of encouragement, acts of kindness, and thoughtfulness.

And it makes me want to do the same for others.

When my debut novel was released, I wanted to do something tangible to help those who have served our country in the armed forces. I looked into donating a portion of the proceeds from book sales to a worthy organization that helps veterans. There were many, but it was Tomorrows Hope that captured my heart.

A dollar from the sale of each autographed copy of *The Heart Remembers*, which is dedicated "to all who served in Vietnam," was donated to the transitional housing and service center located in Coalport, Pa., that provides shelter and basic necessities to homeless veterans. (For more information about Tomorrows Hope, visit their website, found online at http://tomorrowshopepa.org/)

William Penn once said, "I expect to pass through life but once. If therefore, there be any kindness I can show, or any good thing I can do to any fellow being, let me do it now, and not defer or neglect it, as I shall not pass this way again."

O Lord, show me ways that I can pass along Your loving kindness to others today. Amen.

MORE TEA: Read and reflect on Isaiah 54:8, 10.

L: A Loving God Love Notes

Thy steadfast love, O LORD, extends to the heavens, thy faithfulness to the clouds. – Psalm 36:5 RSV

God is love, and he who abides in love abides in God, and God in him. – 1 John 4:16 NKJV

MY FIRST HIGH SCHOOL boyfriend, a tall, skinny basketball player nicknamed "Rebo" (short for "rebound"—his job on the court) was the first boy in high school who liked me back. Finally, I got love notes like the other girls. I was loved! Oh, joy! For Valentine's Day he gave me a huge stuffed St. Bernard that took up nearly half my single bed. I named it "Rebo." (Duh.)

Our romance lasted three months. On the day of our class picnic, on the bus ride home, he handed me a note and told me not to read it until I got home.

It was a "Dear Michele" letter.

I was devastated. I mean, I finally get a boy to like me back, and he dumps me for a cheerleader!

I grieved all summer, sitting in the dark living room on the hardwood floor in front of the stereo, listening to Bobby Vinton and all those emo songs back then. I didn't think I'd ever run out of tears or that my heart, shattered in a million pieces, would ever be whole again.

Then one summer evening, I went to a church bazaar with friends, including the boy who became my high school sweetheart. It was the last night of the event, and the magical August night sky blossomed with fireworks to end the evening.

Well, that was the *first* display of fireworks that night. The second was when I arrived home after walking my best friend, who lived across town, home. I should have called when we got to Kathie's house. (Remember, no cell phones existed back then.)

It was after midnight when I climbed the front porch steps. My father, who'd never gotten angry with me before, met me at the door—not unruffled and quiet, like he usually was. After our heated exchange, I stormed to my room, grounded for two weeks.

I treated Dad with icy silence the next day, Sunday. Monday he left for work. He traveled for his job and would be gone a week.

Wednesday I received a letter.

"My dear Michele," Dad wrote, "Perhaps by now you are over the mad spell at me for scolding you."

It had been the first time I'd ever stayed out late without calling, he explained.

"I was sick with worry after walking up to the bazaar and not finding you there," he wrote. "By that time I was imagining everything."

Mom told me he'd ventured out in his pajamas, poking through the bushes along the way.

"It is so hard for a parent to be cross with a child," he concluded, "But sometimes it is necessary for your own good. Perhaps when you have children of your own, you will understand how we feel."

My icy heart melted. One moment of panic, I realized, doesn't cancel out years of steadfast love. I clutched the letter to my heart, tears once more filling my eyes. But this time they were tears of joy.

Love notes. I think my father's trumps over them all.

Thank You, Father God, for Your steadfast, faithful, and unfailing love. And thank You for the Bible, Your love note to me. Amen.

MORE TEA: Read and reflect on Romans 8:31–39.

M: Majestic God

The heavens declare the glory of God; the skies proclaim the work of His hands. – Psalm 19:1 NIV

LORD, our Lord, how majestic is your name in all the earth! You have set your glory in the heavens. – Psalm 8:1 NIV

I'VE LONG BEEN A sky watcher. As a child, I liked to lie on my back in the yard on a summer day, watching the clouds float across a sapphire sky. As a young mother, after the supper dishes were done, I'd sit on the patio in the evening as twilight deepened and watch the stars come out. It was then, as an adult, I learned to recognize the Big Dipper and the Little Dipper.

I love to watch the sky as a storm moves in. And rainbows! One summer morning when the kids were little, I roused them out of their comfy beds to see a neon rainbow arching in the sky above the house.

And sunsets! Oh, joy! I'll stop in the middle of making supper to gaze at a blazing winter sunset. And once in a while I'll catch the rose blush of a morning sky just before the sun rises. One fall morning the sky cast a copper glow over everything.

To paraphrase the psalmist, When I consider the heavens, the finger-work of God, the moon and the stars, which He set in place (Psalm 8:3) . . . Abraham Lincoln once said, "I can see how it might be possible for a man to look down upon the earth and be an atheist, but I cannot conceive how he could look up into the heavens and say there is no God."

Indeed, "The heavens declare the glory of God, the skies proclaim the work of His hands" (Psalm 19:1 NIV). The sky—the heavens—tell us much about their creator, if only we would *selah*—pause and calmly think about it.

I once heard a scientist give a talk about how nature reflects the Triune God. First, all three—Father, Son, and Holy Spirit—were present and active in creation (Genesis 1:1–5). Three lights were created: the sun ("the greater light to rule the day"), the moon ("the lesser light to rule the night"), and the stars.

Then there's the atom, the basic unit that makes up all matter. The atom is comprised of three parts: protons, neutrons ,and electrons. Matter, defined as "anything that takes up space and has mass," comes in three forms: solid, liquid, and gas.

There are three primary colors: red, yellow, and blue. These three pigment colors cannot be made by mixing other colors. Indeed, from them all other colors are made by mixing together various combinations of red, yellow and blue.

Omne trium perfectum—this Latin phrase means "everything that comes in threes is perfect, or every set of three is complete."

All nature bears the signature of its Triune Creator, perfect and complete, lacking nothing. That's why I love the outdoors in every season. That's why I'm a sky watcher.

Take time to watch the sky. Remember: The Heavens declare the glory of God. The skies proclaim His majesty!

Thank You, God, for creating this beautiful world that reflects Your majesty, just for us. Remind me to take time and enjoy it. Amen.

MORE TEA: Read and reflect on Psalm 8; Genesis 1.

N: The Nature of God

And God said to Moses, "I AM WHO I AM." – Exodus 3:14 NKJV

"But who do you say that I am?" – Jesus, as quoted in Matthew 16:13 NKJV

WHEN I FIRST GOT the idea for this series, "The ABC's of knowing God better," I was enthusiastic about using the letters of the alphabet to describe an indescribable God, to catch a glimpse into His many-faceted nature, to delve into Scripture to discover and learn more about the One who calls us to know Him, love Him and serve Him.

As usual with new ideas, I promptly sat down and recorded my ideas, jotting down at least one word for every letter of the alphabet. Well, almost every letter. Two letters had me stumped: N and X. I figured when the time came to write about that letter, I'd have a word.

I didn't.

So I decided to get some feedback from others and posed the question to my Facebook friends: "This year, every other week, I've been focusing on one attribute of God in my weekly columns. I'm going through the alphabet: 'The ABC's of knowing God better.' This week I wrote about the letter M. But the next letter has me stumped: 'N' … What word beginning with 'N' do you think describes God?"

Here's what they said:

"Never-ending love." (Jeanne)

"Near, nurturing." (Ann)

"Ineffable." (Jodie)

"I know this is an 'I' word, but it is silent!" Jodie said and posted a link to the definition. According to the free Miriam-Webster Online Dictionary, *ineffable* means "too great, powerful, beautiful, etc., to be described or expressed." I read further. "Incapable of being expressed in words; not to be uttered."

Intriguing, considering God's name, Yahweh, was written without the vowels in all caps (YHWH) because the Hebrews felt God's name, which reflected His nature, was too holy to be uttered or written out. Even today you'll run across "G-d" instead of God.

And while we're on the topic, the name *Yahweh* (Jehovah) is a form of the verb *to be*, which is translated I AM in Exodus 3:14 when God revealed Himself to Moses. According to the Children's Ministry Resource Bible, it signifies "the present One, He who is." The Amplified Bible translates this verse as "I AM WHO I AM *and* WHAT I AM, *and* I WILL BE WHAT I WILL BE."

Okay, I'm off on a tangent, but I'm an etymology freak and am fascinated with the origin and history of words. There is much in this short verse, "I AM WHO I AM," (actually a proclamation) to meditate on for a lifetime and never quite grasp the full meaning.

Moving on …

Teresa had a list: "near to my heart, never judgmental, never tired of my neediness, most important NOUN in my life! Never-ending, nurturing, nourishing."

New life. (Margo)

Necessary. (Cass)

"The word *new* came to my mind," Sue B. wrote. "He is New every morning! He always has new and wonderful things planned for us."

Harry posted "Nice," and Susan wrote "New creation."

Wow! Ask and you'll receive!

All these are worthy of reflecting on, and you'll find references to each one in the Bible.

What about you? What word beginning with "N" do *you* think describes God?

Dear God, You may be indescribable, but You are not unknowable. You bid us to come to You so You can lavish Your steadfast love and faithfulness on us. How awesome is that? Amen.

MORE TEA: Read and reflect on Job 38–41:11.

O: Omni-God

If I take the wings of the morning, And dwell in the in the uttermost parts of the sea, Even there Your hand shall lead me, And Your right hand shall hold me. – Psalm 139:9–10 NKJV

"I am with you always." – Jesus, as quoted in Matthew 28:20 NKJV

MY HUSBAND AND I were at a fiftieth wedding anniversary celebration when the storm hit. We were on the front porch chatting with family we hadn't seen in a while. The two-year-old daughter of his cousin was playing on the sidewalk when an earsplitting boom of thunder sounded and lightning flashed across the sky—close, too close for comfort.

She ran to the porch crying, passed her mommy, and went straight to my husband, extending her little arms to him in a child's "pick me up" pose. He obliged. Her crying stopped immediately.

He was her hero that day.

I, too, have someone to run to when life's storms rage around me. And not only then. I seem to bother God with all sorts of trivial things—trivial compared to what other folks are going through.

I remember my mother did the same. She'd hang the laundry on the outside clothesline, then look heavenward and say, "Now, don't You let it rain."

So I learned early to take all my cares and anxieties to God (1 Peter 5:7).

That was the one of the foundation blocks of the faith I have today. For throughout my life, I've seen firsthand that He is, indeed, an "Omni God"—omnipresent, omniscient, and omnipotent. ("Omni" means "all, in all ways, without limits.") He is present everywhere, knows everything, and is all-powerful.

In other words, He's hero material—a real hero, not a fictional one you meet in movies and books. But we love our heroes, don't we? Don't we hope, deep inside, that someone like Indiana Jones, Leroy Jethro Gibbs, Rhett Butler, and Benjamin Gates (*National Treasure*) would appear in *our* lives?

We all need a hero.

With Omni-God, we have one.

But the choice is ours: We can run to Him when the thunder booms and the lightning cracks too close for comfort. We can go to Him with the big things and the little things, because anything that concerns us, concerns Him.

Or we can run the other way or ignore Him. Neither of which, by the way, works. He always knows where we are, we can never get away from His presence, and He is more powerful than we are.

Omni-God, though, is a gentleman and will wait until you are ready—like the prodigal son when he "came to himself" (Luke

15:17). And, like the father in that parable, He waits until He sees you, then, no matter what you've done or how long or how far you've strayed, "He will rejoice over you with gladness, He will renew you in his love; He will exult over you with loud singing as on the day of a festival" (Zephaniah 3:17).

Omni-God—Is He *your* hero?

Omni-God, thank You for being there when I come running. Thank You for being my hero. Amen.

MORE TEA: Read and reflect on Psalm 139.

P: Peace-giving God

The L*ORD blesses his people with peace. – Ps. 29:11 NIV*

"Peace I leave with you, My peace I give to you; not as the world gives do I give to you." –Jesus, as quoted in John 14:27 NKJV

THREE DAYS BEFORE MY twentieth birthday, my father died.

I'd been summoned from college, a hundred miles away. This wasn't the first summons.

I'd been watching Dad lose weight for months. Surgery a month earlier hadn't been successful. But Dad and Mom tried to convince me it was an ulcer, not stomach cancer.

The "C" word. Back then, in 1971, it was a death sentence. Especially when you let it go as long as Dad had.

Perhaps my parents didn't want to burden me during a nineteen-credit semester.

But I knew. Deep down I knew. And gnawed with worry. About Dad. About my academic load. I was a semester away from student teaching, a semester away from graduating. I couldn't afford to miss any more classes.

So I visited one of my favorite professors, one of the few who took a personal interest in his students and who'd be honest with me.

"Go home," he said. "Your family is more important. You can always withdraw and take your courses next semester."

He knew what I wasn't ready to face—that my father was dying.

A friend drove me to the hospital. Dad died a few hours later. It was my first experience with death of someone close to me.

I went home that night looking for him. Surely his spirit would come to say goodbye. I looked and looked. A radio mysteriously turned on. Anything.

But nothing. Nothing until Friday morning, the day of his funeral—and my twentieth birthday.

I sensed it before my eyes even opened that morning—a peace so profound, so pervading, so supreme that it was present in every molecule of the air around me and in every cell of my being.

I, who work with words for a living, have no words to describe it. The closest description is what Paul wrote to the Philippians when he described God's peace as "the peace that passes all understanding" (Philippians 4:7).

God's peace transcends anything we can even imagine on this side of heaven.

Forty-eight years have passed. I've been on the mountain. I've trudged through the valleys. I've wrestled with despair. But I never forgot the gift of peace God gave me that day. Indeed, the memory—I can still almost feel that peace—has gotten me through life's challenges.

I've found truth in what Isaiah wrote: "Thou will keep him in perfect peace whose mind is stayed on Thee" (Isaiah 23:3 KJV).

One of God's names is YHWH Shalom, which means "The LORD is peace." He is peace and He gives peace. The peace that transcends all understanding.

Do you have it? Have you asked for it?

May Your peace, O Lord, reign in my heart and soul and mind today and every day. Amen.

MORE TEA: Read and reflect on Mark 4:35–41.

Q: Three Q's of God

So this is what the Sovereign LORD says: "See, I lay a stone in Zion, a tested stone, a precious cornerstone for a sure foundation; the one who relies on it will never be stricken with panic." – Isaiah 28:16 NIV

Jesus said to them, "Have you never read in the Scriptures: 'The stone the builders rejected has become the cornerstone; the Lord has done this, and it is marvelous in our eyes'?" – Matthew 21:42 NIV

"WHAT WAS I THINKING?" I muttered to myself as I mulled over words beginning with the letter Q that describe God.

I browsed through the Q section in a Bible dictionary and my *Flip Dictionary*, which is actually a thesaurus, and came up with three possibilities: qualified, quantity, and quoin.

Qualified means "having the necessary skill, experience, or knowledge to do a particular job or activity: having the qualifications to do something" (Merriam-Webster online dictionary). You could say God, the Creator of all there is, is qualified. He sets the bar. More than that. He *is* the bar. He is the omni of omnis. He can do anything, for nothing is impossible for Him (Luke 1:37, Matthew 19:26).

Quantity, a noun, means "an amount or number of something; a large amount or number of something."

How big is God? Bigger than you or I can imagine. He limitless, infinite. I love the way A.W. Tozer describes this attribute of God: "God, being infinite, does not dwell in space; He swallows up all space. Scripture says, 'Do not I fill heaven and earth?' (Jeremiah 23:24), and that sounds as if God were contained in heaven and earth. But actually God fills heaven and earth just as the ocean fills a bucket which has been submerged in it a mile down. The bucket is full of ocean, but the ocean surrounds the bucket in all directions." (*The Attributes of God)*

Then I came to quoin. What's a quoin and why would I choose such an odd word to describe God?

Actually it's quite appropriate.

Wikipedia describes quoins as "masonry blocks at the corner of a wall. They exist in some cases to provide actual strength for a wall made with inferior stone or rubble."

A quoin is like a cornerstone—"the stone representing the starting place in the construction of a monumental building"—and a keystone—"the wedge-shaped piece at the crown of an arch that locks the other pieces in place; something that is essential, indispensable, or basic." (Dictionary.com)

"See," God tells us through the prophet Isaiah, "I lay a stone in Zion, a chosen and precious cornerstone, and the one who trusts in him will never be put to shame" (Isaiah 28:16).

I thought finding a word beginning with the letter Q to describe God was impossible.

Then God showed me nothing with the One who fills time and space and gives strength to inferior rubble like me is impossible.

Thank You, infinite God, for being my cornerstone, my rock of stability, in a world that gets more instable by the day. Amen.

MORE TEA: Read and reflect on Psalm 118.

R: A Place of Refuge

I will say of the LORD, "He is my refuge and my fortress." – Psalm 91:2 NIV

"Come with me by yourselves to a quiet place and get some rest."– Jesus, as quoted in Mark 6:31 NIV

WHEN MY PARENTS BOUGHT the rustic one-room cabin in the western Pennsylvania mountains, my mother dubbed it Camp St. Jude after the saint of impossible cases.

I don't think she was as fired up about buying the property as my father was. Dad wanted a guy place where he could hunt and enjoy the peace only a place like this could offer. It was the polar opposite of the life we lived in Donora, one of the steel mill towns along the Monongahela River.

Camp St. Jude had no water or electric, only gas-fueled sconces on the wall, a kerosene lantern on the table, a wood-burning stove (which we named "Hot Stuff") in the middle of the yellowed linoleum floor, and an outhouse, which we called "the poogie house" (rhymes with "cookie").

To convince Mom to buy the place, Dad treated us to a week in a log cabin in Cook Forest—the first family vacation I remember—and promised Mom electricity, running water, an addition so the five of us wouldn't be crawling on top of each other, and a foundation of concrete block instead of the piers it stood on.

The next several summers were spent fulfilling that promise, although the only running water we obtained was from the neighbor's well, which we pumped by hand and carted back in a wagon along a swampy path in five-gallon, galvanized milk cans.

But we had fun. Fun yanking nails out of old siding, ripping off the roof, holding lumber in place while Dad sawed. Fun imagining branches were horses, fun pretending we were space travelers and the wooden swing hanging between two big pine trees was a space ship from Mars. I spent hours in the boughs of a big pine on the corner of the property where I dreamed of what my life would be like when I grew up.

And then I grew up. My husband and I sold Camp St. Jude when I was pregnant with our third child. Close friends bought it and, over the years, remodeled it. One summer they invited Dean and me to spend a weekend there with them.

Camp St. Jude hadn't lost its magic. I awoke Saturday morning refreshed and relaxed. I couldn't remember when I'd slept that well.

It is still a place of refuge, a place to go when the world is just too much to bear, when the stress stretches me to a breaking point, when I feel overwhelmed and in too deep. Perhaps that's what Dad saw when he first set eyes on the place.

I can't always go to Camp St. Jude when life gets a little too much, but I can go to God. He is more than "the saint of impossible cases." He can make the impossible possible.

Thank You, Father God, that I can run to You for refuge any time. Amen.

MORE TEA: Read and reflect on Psalm 91.

S: Shepherd God

We are His people and the sheep of His pasture. – Psalm 100:14 NKJV

"I am the Good Shepherd." – Jesus, as quoted in Philippians 4:13 NIV

SHEEP ARE MENTIONED IN the Bible more than five hundred times, more than any other animal. This shouldn't be too surprising, as sheep were important to the agricultural life of the Hebrews.

But sheep are also used symbolically to refer to God's people. Have you ever wondered why?

First of all, sheep are natural followers. Their instinct is to follow the sheep in front of them. When one sheep decides to wander off, the rest of the flock usually follows. Unlike other animals, they are led, not driven. That's why the shepherd goes before them. If the shepherd were to go behind them, the flock would scatter.

Second, sheep are sociable creatures, living in flocks, staying together while grazing. There's safety in numbers, as predators are less likely to pounce on a group than one solitary, wayward sheep. However, sheep are known to wander from the fold and have no sense of direction when they get lost (sounds like me). When cornered, their instinct is to flee, not fight. Indeed, they don't have the equipment to fight—no sharp teeth or hooves, for example—and they can't run very fast. So a lone sheep separated from the flock is a sheep in trouble.

Third, sheep can easily become downcast, and if not tended to right away, can die quickly or become dinner for a predator. In his book, *A Shepherd Looks at the 23rd Psalm*, former shepherd turned lay pastor Phillip Keller describes what it means when a sheep is downcast: "This is an old English shepherd's term for a sheep that has turned over on its back and cannot get up again by itself. (It is not strong enough.) . . . It is so essential for the shepherd to look over his flock every day, counting them to see that all are able to be up and on their feet."

Sheep are easily frightened and will stampede, which can lead to them piling up against each other and smothering. Sheep will not drink from running water, so the shepherd must find still waters for them to drink from. They never walk in a straight line (me again) and are the only animals that need care 24/7. And, unlike horses and dogs (and probably more like cats), they're not trainable.

But sheep have good traits, too. Their excellent senses, for instance. They recognize and remember faces and their own shepherd's voice. At night several flocks could be housed together in one pen, but when morning comes, all the shepherd has to do to separate his flock from the rest is to call out to his sheep, and they will follow him out of the pen.

The shepherd's job is to protect and defend his sheep, seek those that wander away. He must know his sheep well, minister to their wounds, rescue them, lead them, all the while being gentle with them.

And he never leaves his sheep alone. His abiding presence is their safety, their security, and their salvation.

Does any of this sound familiar?

We are the sheep of God's pasture. He will take care of each of us as a good shepherd takes care of his sheep.

Thank You, Father, for watching over and taking care of a dumb sheep like me. Amen.

MORE TEA: Read and reflect on John 10:1–18; Psalm 23.

T: God Is Truth

And the L*ORD passed by before him, and proclaimed, "The* L*ORD, the* L*ORD God, merciful and gracious, longsuffering, and abundant in goodness and truth." – Exodus 34:6 NIV*

"I am the way, the truth, and the life." – Jesus, as quoted in John 14:6 NKJV

I'VE ALWAYS BEEN ONE to believe whatever anyone told me. Call me gullible. Call me naïve, but I'm a trusting soul.

My mother taught me to always tell the truth, even if it got me into trouble. Like the time my brother, sister, cousin Billy, and I were playing in the backyard, where a green canvas Army tent stood. When my mother called my siblings inside for a few minutes, Billy decided to hide from them.

"Don't tell them where I am," he said as he slipped into the tent.

"I won't," I said, feeling awesome that my older cousin trusted me—the youngest of the family—with such important information.

When they returned, I put on the most solemn expression I could and said, "Billy isn't in the tent."

I've never been able to lie, and I figured everyone else was wired the same way.

But I discovered, to my pain, they aren't.

Like the time my high school boyfriend slipped me a note on the bus coming home from the class picnic at the end of the school year and whispered, "No matter what happens, always remember I love you."

Yeah, right. The note was a "Dear Michele" letter. But I clung to his spoken words throughout that miserable summer even though my heart was broken. Just before the new school year began, I learned he dumped me for a cheerleader.

But it didn't sour me on people.

Then in college I got burned again. I was in the dorm lobby with my then-fiancé (who at least told me the truth when he dumped me a year later) waiting for one of the girls in the group I hung around with to return from an errand. It was her birthday, and we'd planned a surprise party. Tammy, one of the gang, told me she'd let me know when the birthday girl came.

So when Tammy came down and said Penny hadn't returned yet but she'd come get me when she did, I had no reason not to believe her. Turns out she lied. Penny *had* returned. Tammy went up to the party and told everyone I didn't want to come. And I wondered for the longest time why I suddenly didn't have any friends.

As a teacher, I learned students were adept at lying—no hint whatever of deceit in their eyes.

I'm sure glad there is one person I know who will never lie—because He can't. It's not in His nature.

“God is not human, that he should lie,” Scripture tells us (Numbers 23:19). He is “abundant in truth” (Exodus 34:6), “a faithful God, without deceit” (Deuteronomy 52:4) and “the God of truth” (Isaiah 65:16). The apostle Paul called Him “the ever truthful God Who cannot deceive” (Titus 1:2).

People will deceive us. But God never will.

And that’s a truth I can stake my life on.

Thank You, God, that I can trust what You say and know that You will never break Your promises. Amen.

MORE TEA: Read and reflect on Psalm 119:41–48.

U: A God Who Understands

Do you not know? Have you not heard? The Lord *is the everlasting God, the Creator of the ends of the earth. He will not grow tired or weary, and his understanding no one can fathom. – Isaiah 40:28 NIV*

Everyone who heard him was amazed at his understanding and his answers. – Luke 2:47 NIV

ONE OF THE DEEPEST longings we have as human beings is to be understood. If someone truly understands us—who we are deep inside, why we act and react the way we do—and remains in our lives, we know that person loves us, warts and all.

I've been blessed to have such persons in my life.

First there were my parents, who understood me a lot better than I thought they did. They watched me as I matured, had a hand in developing who I became, and saw parts of themselves in me.

Then there was my godmother, my precious Aunt Betty, who understood me better than my own mother did. While Mom gave me practical birthday gifts, Aunt Betty gave me the girly things I longed for.

Then there's my husband, whose understanding of me has grown with time. He's seen me frantic, worried, angry, afraid, anxious, joyful—the gamut of emotions. How blessed I am that he's hung around all these years. He understands me through and through—and loves me still.

Then there's my friend Sharon, who understands me because we share both a sisterhood in our womanhood and a common bond as believers. She understands me because we've spent time together, and she's listened to me with not only her ears but also with her heart. She understands me because I've trusted her enough to let down my guard and allow her to see me as I really am.

But there's Someone who understands me even better than anyone, even better than I understand myself—my heavenly Father, my Creator.

Psalm 139, one of my favorite portions of Scripture, plumbs the depths of God's loving understanding of each of us. You are not a nameless face in the mass of humanity. You are His child, uniquely created, intensely loved, and thoroughly understood.

He knows you better than you know yourself. He knows when you come and when you go, when you sit, when you lie down and when you rise. He knows what you think and what you're going to say before you even say it (vv. 1–3).

No matter where you go, He is with you, ready to guide you when you need direction and ready to hold you fast when you need stability and security. And when you're scared of the dark, His eyes pierce the darkness—for darkness is as light to Him (vv. 5–12).

He saw you before you were born (vv. 15–16). He shaped you inside and out. Body and soul, you are marvelously made (vv. 3–4, The Message).

Each day of your life had a plan and a purpose even before you took your first breath (v. 16).

He thinks about you constantly—so much you cannot even begin to fathom how much (vv. 17–18).

So the next time you're feeling misunderstood, when you think no one could possibly understand you, remember the One who created you and, more than anyone else, knows you, understands you, and loves you, warts and all.

Abba Father, how awesome to be understood and loved like You understand and love me! Amen.

MORE TEA: Read and reflect on Psalm 139.

V: I Am the Vine
Staying Connected

And the LORD God formed man of the dust of the ground, and breathed into his nostrils the breath of life; and man became a living being. – Genesis 2:7 NKJV

"I am the vine, you are the branches. . . Without Me you can do nothing." – John 15:5 NKJV

I LEARNED TO TYPE on a big, black, heavy, manual typewriter. I composed many a poem on that old machine, using half-sheets of erasable-bond typing paper and saving them in a handkerchief box.

When I got to college, my roommate let me use her portable electric typewriter—and I fell in love! With just a slight touch of the keys, sentences zoomed across the page. (Although I did have to learn not to press so hard.) I begged for one for Christmas, and Santa obliged. I used that machine for over twenty-five years, typing tests, quizzes, and worksheets on mimeograph masters in my teaching days.

About the time I began writing seriously and submitting my articles to magazines, I learned of something called a word processor. It was like an electric typewriter with a screen (monitor), and I didn't have to use erasable bond typing paper or whiteout or scratch my mistakes off the page with a razor blade. All I had to do was use the delete key. My work was saved to a floppy disk (remember those?), as the word processor had no internal memory to store documents.

I was happy with my Brother word processor, even when I began using a computer at the newsroom where I worked as a feature writer. Although I saw the advantages, I resisted the idea of getting a personal computer. After all, my word processor never crashed.

Eventually, though, I caved in. Why had I waited so long? My word processor was relegated to the attic beside the electric typewriter.

I resisted, however, connecting to the Internet—too much risk, I thought, after hearing stories about viruses and hackers and other such boogeymen of the information superhighway.

It took me a while to cave in on that one. But cave in I did, going from a dialup connection through my phone line to a satellite dish on the side of my house.

Progress.

From an ugly old manual typewriter to a sleek laptop. From limited telephone communication to being able to connect with anyone on the planet at any time. From boxes and file cabinet drawers stuffed with file folders and floppy disks to practically unlimited online storage space in what's called a cloud.

But just let the electricity go out, and we're stymied. We can use our laptops, portable devices, and cell phones until the batteries die, then we're helpless until the power comes back on.

To get anything accomplished these days, it seems, it's vital to remain connected to an electric power source.

"I am the vine, you are the branches," Jesus said. "He who abides in Me, and I in Him, bears much fruit; for without Me you can do nothing" (John 15:5).

Just as I wouldn't want to go back to the days I used a cumbersome manual typewriter, I don't want to go back to the time I lived my life without Jesus, my personal power source that never goes out.

Remind me, Lord, to stay plugged in—that in You "I live and move and have my being" (Acts 17:28). Amen.

MORE TEA: Read and reflect on John 15:1–15.

W: Wise God
A Heart of Wisdom

Teach us to number our days, that we may gain a heart of wisdom. – Psalm 90:12 NIV

If any of you lacks wisdom, you should ask God, who gives generously to all without finding fault, and it will be given to you. – James 1:5 NIV

HENRIETTA BENSON WAS THE wisest person I've ever known.

When I met her, I was a young mother with three children, the third of which was unplanned. I was quite upset about it. I was, truth be told, mad at God.

Back then I was still under the illusion that life should go according to what I'd planned, what I'd worked for, what I'd prayed for. But God had things to teach me, and I was at times a reluctant, if not rebellious, learner. Impatience was one of my defining traits—and perfectionism. I worried about what others would think or say about me or my family. If my kids did something wrong, somehow it was my fault.

Enter Henrietta Benson: mother, grandmother, and great-grandmother; former teacher in a one-room schoolhouse; farm wife; godly woman. Once Henrietta and her family began attending our little church on Canoe Ridge, I was never the same.

Henrietta's philosophy was that once she met you, you were family. Not only were there church functions, such as carry-in dinners for Mother's Day, Father's Day, Thanksgiving, and other holidays, there were also picnics and campouts on the hill, part of the farmland she and her husband owned.

So there were plenty of opportunities for me to pour my heart out to her. She'd listen patiently, keeping her eyes and attention on me, never interrupting, with not even a sliver of judgment on her face or in her eyes. Some folks you can't talk to—you can't reveal the pain, the worry, the mistakes, how you really feel, the stuff that makes up the real you—the things you hide from the world because you don't want anyone to think less of you.

Henrietta never preached. She'd wait until I finished my tirade then, like soothing balm on a seeping wound, dispensed her words of wisdom. They were few, but they were effective.

I can't remember specifically the words she said—after all, my children are all grown and gone now. But I can remember how she made me feel—understood, loved, and accepted as I was; that I wasn't hopeless; that God was using these things to change me and make me into the person He planned for me to be.

She taught me more about God and what He is like than any Bible study or sermon ever did.

Looking back on it all now, I realize that oftentimes it wasn't I who sought her—it was she who drew me out with a "You look stressed today, Michele."

Henrietta has long left this world for her heavenly home, but her godly influence and wisdom live on. You see, now it's my turn to be a listening ear, give a timely word of wisdom, dispense love unconditionally.

It's my time to pass it forward.

Thank You, Father, for Henrietta and her godly wisdom. Grant me the grace, love, and wisdom to be to others what she was to me. Amen.

MORE TEA: Read and reflect on Proverbs 2.

X: X-travagant God

The steadfast love of the L*ORD* *never ceases, his mercies never come to an end; they are new every morning; great is thy faithfulness. –Lamentations 3:21–23 RSV*

Every good and perfect gift is from above, coming down from the Father of the heavenly lights, who does not change like shifting shadows. – James 1:17 NIV

"HOW MUCH ARE YOU spending on me for Christmas this year?" my husband asked me one year before the holiday.

I didn't want to tell him I'd already ordered everything on his list. His list, by the way, is comprised of dog-eared pages in several Cabela's catalogs with which we get inundated at this time of the year.

So while DH was out vainly looking for a first day buck, I was online not so vainly spending bucks. I was supposed to spend only a third of what I did—that's what he says he's spending on me. But trying to pick and choose is too agonizing. It's a lot easier just to get everything.

This seems to be our Christmas history—well, mine, anyway, because I'm the one who did the Christmas shopping all those years.

When the kids were little, I tried to get everything on their lists, too. The money was short, but seeing the look on their faces when they opened their presents on Christmas morning was a gift of its own. I wanted to be as extravagant as our budget allowed.

We have a heavenly Father who wants to be extravagant with His children, too. Only He can afford to lavish every good gift upon us—and He does. Oh, we don't get everything on our wish list, but He gives us exactly what we need when we need it and in His way.

Some of His gifts we don't even think about. Or maybe we don't even realize we've been given them.

Take, for example, His *love*. It reaches to the heavens (Ps. 36:5), surrounds us (Ps. 32:10), never ceases (Lamentations 3:22), and is the reason He sent His Son to provide the way to heaven for us (John 3:16).

His *faithfulness* shields us (Ps. 91:4), extends to the clouds (Ps. 36:5) and continues through all generations (Ps. 119:90).

His unlimited *mercies*—we receive them daily, fresh as the morning dew (Lamentations 3:22–23).

He supplies all our *needs*, and He doesn't skimp, either. He provides them according to His glorious riches (Philippians 4:19). Wow! All we have to do is ask (Matthew 7:7).

His *grace*, which is His daily care, strength, guidance, and favor. His grace is all we really need, for what we lack, He provides (2 Corinthians 12:9).

His *wisdom*—Once again, all we have to do is ask: "If any of you lacks wisdom he should ask God, who gives generously to all, without finding fault, and it will be given to you" (James 1:5).

Did you get that? He gives *generously to all.*

So go ahead. Make up that wish list—then watch your heavenly Father do what He loves to do—be extravagant with His child.

Forgive me, Father, when I whine and complain that I don't have enough or I don't have what I want. Open my eyes to the gifts You shower me with every day. Amen.

NOTE: For more examples of God's extravagance, read about the miracles of the loaves and the fishes and see how many baskets of leftovers were gathered up (Matthew 14:13–21 and 15:32–38). Or the miraculous catches of fish in Luke 5:4–7 and John 21:4–6.

MORE TEA: Read and reflect on Matthew 7:7–11.

Y: YHWH
LORD of All

God also said to Moses, "Say this to the Israelites: Yahweh, the God of your fathers ... has sent me to you. This is My name forever." –Exodus 3:15 HCSB

"She will give birth to a son, and you are to name him Yeshua, [which means 'ADONAI saves,'] because he will save his people from their sins." – Matthew 1:21 CJB

MY MOTHER WANTED TO name me Teresa, but my dad disagreed. "Her name is Michele," he said.

And so it was. That is, until someone came along and called me "Mickey."

"Don' t call her that. It might stick."

And so it did.

I don't know who said what in giving me my nickname, but until high school only family members called me Mickey. In school I was Michele. One "l." Please.

When I got to high school, I determined *Michele* wasn't cool enough, but so I changed the spelling of my nickname to Mikki. Which I thought was cool.

So my high school peers still call me Mikki.

On to college. Mikki just wasn't sophisticated enough, so I went back to Michele. One "l." Please.

And stayed with it.

When I started teaching, I was "Miss Maddock." Halfway through my second year I became "Mrs. Huey."

A few years later I became "Mommy." I was already "Aunt Michele."

Then twenty years ago another name was added—Grandma.

I wear my names with pride. Each one indicates not only who I am and who I belong to, it conveys relationship and position.

God's names, too, indicate relationship and position, as well as His divine attributes.

It would take a tome to discuss all God's names and what they mean, but I'd like to focus on a few that have a personal meaning to me.

First and foremost, God is YHWH. The divine name He gave to Moses when Moses asked Him what should he tell the Israelites when they asked, "What is His name?" (Exodus 3:13).

"I AM WHO I AM," God replied. Which translates *Yahweh*, or *YHWH* since the Israelites considered God's name to be too holy to say aloud.

Yahweh is a form of the verb "to be," which is translated in this verse *I AM.*

The English rendering of YHWH is LORD and is found over seven thousand times in Scripture. It means "Self-existence or Eternal One," "The One who exists because of who He is, and speaks of His holiness, justice, and hatred of sin. ("Names of God," *Children's Ministry Resource Bible*, p. 914)

Other names of God that have a personal meaning to me include:

El Shaddai – "Almighty God." Strength, lifegiver, the bountiful supplier of all blessings also are included in the meaning of El Shaddai. He gives me life, strength, and abundant blessings.

YHWH Yireh – "The-LORD-will-provide." He provides for all my needs.

YHWH Shalom – "The-LORD-Is-Peace." Only God can give me inner peace.

YHWH Rophe – "The-LORD-Who-Heals." God restores, strengthens, and heals me.

YHWH Roii – "The LORD Our Shepherd." With tenderness, God cares for, guides, and protects me, like a shepherd cares for his flock.

My personal favorite is the name Hagar gave to God when He met her in the wilderness after she fled the abusive Sarah: *Lahai Roi*, "You-Are-the-God-Who-Sees." To God she was more than a slave, a servant, a foreigner. She was a person He cared for enough to meet her at her lowest point and meet her deepest need. To Him, she was not invisible. (Genesis 16)

And then there's *Yeshua*, more commonly *Jesus*—"The LORD is salvation," or "ADONAI saves."

Which of God's names have a personal meaning for you? Why?

Thank You, YHWH, for all that You are to me. Amen.

NOTE: The names for God and their meanings were taken from the *Children's Ministry Resource Bible* © 1993 by Child Evangelism Fellowship, Inc.

MORE TEA: Read and reflect on Exodus 3:13–15.

Z: Zealous God
A God with Gusto

He put on righteousness as a breastplate, and a helmet of salvation on his head; he put on garments of vengeance for clothing, and wrapped himself in zeal as a cloak. –Isaiah 59:17 ESV

His disciples remembered that it was written, "Zeal for your house will consume me." –John 2:17 ESV

ZEAL. WHAT, EXACTLY, IS IT?

One online dictionary defines it as "great energy or enthusiasm in pursuit of a cause or objective." Synonyms include passion, fervor, and gusto.

You don't hear the word *zeal* used too much today. I wonder if the intensity of the word and its meaning cause people to back off. I mean, another synonym is committedness, root word commit. When you commit yourself to something or someone, you determine to see it through to the end, come what may.

Take marriage, for instance. When you pledge to become one until "death do us part," you make a commitment to your spouse that you'll work together to stay together come what may—sickness and health, poverty and prosperity, good times and bad times—you vow to love and cherish your mate for better or worse for the rest of your lives.

Promises made are only as good as promises kept. Life happens, people change, and love wanes, and we don't fight for it. Like tending a garden, in order to survive the droughts, the storms, the scorching temperatures, the freezing ones, the bugs, the blights, the bunnies and other critters, you must be diligent at consistently nurturing, cultivating, and protecting it.

That's where zeal comes in.

I use marriage here as an example, but other pursuits in life also thrive on zeal. Like rearing children, getting an education, learning a new skill, pursuing a career, developing God-given talents, helping others.

What does this have to do with God?

The Bible describes Him as a zealous God. Some translations use the word *jealous*, but that word has too many negative connotations.

God is zealous for His children—for you, for me. He is committed to us with a love that is unconditional, meaning it doesn't depend on what we say or do or how we feel. We can run as far away from Him as we want (well, we can try), but we will never outrun His presence, His provision, His protection, and His love.

We are the cause, the objective He pursues with passion, fervor, and gusto. Why?

Simply this: He loves us.

He loves us so much that He gave us a free will to decide for ourselves whether we want to return that love or reject it. He loves us so much that He hates the sin that separates us from Him. He loves us so much that He sent His own Son to take the punishment for that sin so that we can be with Him forever in the place He's prepared for us.

Imagine a father standing over the crib of his sleeping child. That's God standing over us. In the words of the prophet Zephaniah, "The Lord your God in your midst, The Mighty One, will save; He will rejoice over you with gladness, He will quiet you with His love, He will rejoice over you with singing" (Zephaniah 3:17 NKJV).

No matter what. Come what may.

He is zealous for you.

My mind just can't wrap around that kind of love, O God. But I am so thankful for it. Indeed, I can't exist without it. As Your child, may I inherit a portion of Your zeal, so that I may reflect You to the world around me. Amen.

MORE TEA: Read and reflect on Zephaniah 3:17.

Aging with Grace

We have this treasure in jars of clay.

–2 Corinthians 4:7 NIV

The Girl in the Picture

So we do not lose heart. Though our outward nature is wasting away, our inner nature is being renewed every day. –2 Corinthians 4:16 RSV

EVERY YEAR FOR NEARLY thirty years my husband and I attended a holiday dinner given by his employers. One year, when the children were still at home and the job list longer than the day (and my energy supply), the dinner was held at a fashionable, classy country club. No longer was I the slim, young thing pictured in a snapshot my husband keeps in his wallet. The years had brought with them a few more pounds and put a dent in the youthful self-esteem exuding from the photo I sometimes wish he'd stop showing to everybody.

There were other changes, too: The long, silky, chestnut hair that cascaded over the bare shoulders of the girl in the picture, taken on the day she got engaged, was now cropped short. With a husband, three children, and a house to take care of, she no longer had the time for herself.

That evening, however, I'd taken extra care getting dressed, and, when I came down the stairs, I was compliment-ready. But my spouse only glanced at the clock and said, "We'd better get going. I don't want to be late."

He said little on the one-hour drive in the swirling snow to the country club, but I was feeling too good to let his silence ruin my mood. Besides, the evening was still young.

When we arrived at the country club, we turned up the long, curved driveway that led to the hilltop restaurant. As we neared the portico, he asked, in an attempt to be thoughtful, "Do you want me to drop you off here?"

"Sure," I said, opening the car door.

At that moment, the headlights illuminated a large sign: "BAG DROP."

We're all growing older. We're changing physically, mentally, emotionally, and spiritually. Shifts occur in our social life, too, as the people we associate with change, move away, experience life-altering health problems, or pass away. Some of the changes we've looked forward to, but others, such as weight gain and health issues, are more difficult to deal with. I don't want to turn into a crotchety, bitter old person. I'd rather age with grace. With all the changes, wanted and unwanted, that getting older brings, how *do* we age with grace?

Aging with grace just doesn't happen on its own. Like everything else worthwhile in life, it must attained through planning and conscientious effort.

The girl in the picture still exists—deep down in the heart of a sixty-eight-year-old grandmother who's learned the secret to a happy life despite the aches and pains that age brings: "Though our outward nature is wasting away, our inner nature is being renewed every day" (2 Corinthians 4:16).

Someone once wrote, "You can take no credit for beauty at sixteen. But if you are beautiful at sixty, it will be your soul's own doing."

Lord, help me to be beautiful on the inside, where it really counts. Amen.

MORE TEA: Read and reflect on 2 Corinthians 4:16–18.

Growing New Wood

They will still bear fruit in old age, they will stay fresh and green. – Psalm 92:14 NIV

"I WILL NOT MAKE age an issue," the late Ronald Reagan said in 1984, when, at age seventy-three, he was running for the US Presidency. "I am not going to exploit for political purposes my opponent's youth and inexperience."

His opponent was fifty-six.

Life doesn't end at sixty or sixty-two or sixty-five, or whatever age the government or company you work for says you must retire. You can still produce in the autumn and winter seasons of life.

Vanderbilt increased his fortune by $100 million between the ages of seventy and eighty-three. When he was seventy-four, Verdi composed his masterpiece, *Othello*; when he was eighty, *Falstaff*; and when he was eighty-five, the *Ave Maria*. Cato began to study Greek when he was eighty, the same age that Goethe wrote *Faust*. At eighty-three Tennyson penned his renowned poem, "Crossing the Bar." And at ninety-eight, Titian created his historic painting, "The Battle of Lepanto."

Productivity in the golden years isn't only for the ancients, either. I knew a man who went deep sea fishing when he was ninety-one.

What's the secret to aging with grace? The first secret is to keep growing. Anything that isn't growing is dead.

"That tree is very old, but I never saw prettier blossoms on it than it now bears," Henry Wadsworth Longfellow once wrote. "That tree grows new wood every year. Like that apple tree, I try to grow a little new wood every year."

We, too, need to grow a little new wood each year. The Bible tells us that "Jesus grew in wisdom and stature, and in favor with God and man" (Luke 2:52). That means He grew mentally, physically, spiritually, and socially. So should we, no matter what our age.

"Be transformed by the renewing of your mind," Paul wrote (Romans 12:2). Grow mentally by keeping your mind active. Learn something new. Read something that requires effort, thought, and concentration, such as classic literature. Take a continuing education course. Write your memoirs, research your genealogy and family history. Do crossword puzzles or solve brain teasers. Play games that require thinking, such as Scrabble or Scattergories.

Physically, our bodies are no longer growing as they did when we were young, but they still need upkeep. I call it "temple keeping" because God's Word tells me my body is a temple of the Holy Spirit (1 Corinthians 3:16–17, 6:19–20). So I take care of this temple by eating right, getting the proper amount of rest, and exercising regularly (well, I try). It's important to know my limits and pay attention to what my temple is telling me. Taking care of health issues immediately will save me a lot of grief and hassle down the road. And I keep up appearances because if I look good, I feel good, and if I feel good, I do good.

The famous comic strip artist Harry Hershfield lived a fruitful life until his death in 1974 at the age of eighty-nine.

"I wake up every morning at eight a.m. and reach for the morning paper," he once said. "Then I look at the obituary page. If my name's not in it, I *get up*!"

Lord, show me ways I can grow a little new wood every day. Amen.

MORE TEA:

Read and reflect on 2 Corinthians 4:16–18; Psalm 92:12–14.

Hush Hour

Even to your old age and gray hairs I am he, I am he who will sustain you. I have made you and I will carry you. –Isaiah 46:4 NIV

ONE OF THE THINGS I liked about teaching school was summer vacation. It wasn't so much that I got to sleep in—because I tried to keep the same wake-sleep schedule as I had during the school year. It was the expanded quiet time for devotions that I most enjoyed.

From September to June I was lucky to have a half an hour a day to read my Bible and pray, let alone delve into spiritual growth books, work through an in-depth Bible study, and keep a spiritual journal. I didn't even think about those "read the Bible in one year" schedules. I simply didn't have the time. My prayers were usually said during the half-hour drive to work. And I just didn't have the mental or physical energy in the evening to attend a Bible study, as much as I wanted to.

During the summer, however, I had no reason to get out the door at a certain time. Taking at least two hours for devotions, for me, was the next thing to heaven. Perhaps that was one reason I felt so good during the summer—I wasn't so fatigued or stressed. Blanketing the day with prayer and plunging deeply into the Word help me to cope when life comes at me fast.

In their book *The Graying of America*, Donald H. and Barry C. Kauser note that people with faith tend to live longer: "Does religion actually serve to improve the health of elderly people? Over ten years of studies at various universities have indicated that … people who have a deep religious faith seem to get sick less often and get better faster when they do get sick than people with much less religious faith. Those with a strong religious faith have also been found to have lower rates of heart disease, stroke and cancer."

An article in the April 2005 issue of *Reader's Digest* reflects a growing conclusion, backed by scientific studies, that "religion and spirituality can reduce stress and boost the immune system" ("The Healing Power of Prayer," p. 153). One study, of AIDS patients, found that "the frequency of prayer was significantly related to longer survival."

"It seemed that people for whom religion had played a major role throughout their lives were aging better than those who weren't religious," one researcher noted.

Aging with grace, then, involves not only keeping active mentally and physically, but also taking your relationship with God to a higher and deeper level through prayer, and reading, studying, and meditating on Scripture.

But that doesn't mean you become a hermit (tempting though it is sometimes). Service is also a key to growing spiritually in the golden years. What wisdom borne of experience and expertise the older generation has to offer the younger!

"Let us consider how we may spur one another on toward love and good deeds. Let us not give up meeting together … but let us encourage one another," the writer of Hebrews instructs. No age limit there.

Serving others gives our lives purpose and meaning in a time when we may start to feel useless and used up. You never retire from God's work. We all know and admire people who, long into their golden years, are still serving, still giving to others.

"The measure of a life, after all, is not its duration, but its donation," said Holocaust survivor Corrie Ten Boom.

My husband is now retired, and I work out of our home as a speaker and writer. Upon rising every morning, we grab our Bibles and head to our Quiet Time places. Rush hour has been replaced by hush hour.

Lord, may I find purpose and fulfillment in my golden years through growing my faith and expanding it in serving others. Amen.

MORE TEA: Read and reflect on John 15:5–8.

Tickle Your Funny Bone

However many years a many may live, let him enjoy them all. – Ecclesiastes 11:8 NIV

I WAS SUCH A fun-loving child. I created ridiculous skits to make others laugh, played impractical jokes, and looked for ways to make everything I did fun. Once I put salt in the sugar bowl and sugar in the saltshaker, then crouched under the table to enjoy the reaction of my unsuspecting victim, which happened to be my mother. Her reaction was enough to convince me not to do that again!

I even found ways to make church fun—for me, anyway. I attended a Catholic grade school, and we started every day with Mass. We first graders got to sit right up front, close to the statue of Mary, Jesus's mother. The statue, I thought, made a great target for my best friend's mittens.

After a couple mitten-tossing episodes, Sister Bertrille, my teacher, decided it would be better if I sat beside her. But that wasn't enough to deter me. When eyes were closed and heads were bent in prayer, I'd reach under the pew and pull off the shoes of the person kneeling in front of me.

Back then, paddling was acceptable, and I made many trips to the supply room, where such discipline was administered. I didn't dare complain to my mother, though. I'd get it twice as bad from her if she found out. For me, though, the fun and laughter were worth the risk of a sore bottom.

Although my way of finding fun was often impractical and annoying (fortunately, I grew out of that stage), I inherently knew the secret to surviving life: Find the fun in everything. A healthy sense of humor is life's best shock absorber.

This is the third secret to aging with grace: Finding joy in every day, in every circumstance. Joy is a choice.

I never like to tell someone to "have a good day." "Have" is so passive, so bland, so blah. It doesn't do anything. It just sits there. I'd rather say, "Enjoy your day." Now enjoy is action we choose.

According to a *Reader's Digest* article titled "I Am Moe's Funny Bone," choosing joy by means of healthy laughter affects our bodies in positive ways: It stimulates the "feel good" chemicals in our brains (what an addiction!), burns calories (and maybe helps us to lose weight?), gives our face a healthy glow (from the increased blood flow), reduces symptoms of stress, increases our resistance to disease and boosts our immune system, increases the oxygen flowing through our system due to the expanded use of our lungs, helps to keep glucose levels in check, reduces clotting and inflammation in the blood vessels, increases our tolerance for pain and, with all the muscles engaged when we laugh, acts as good exercise, especially for folks who physically are unable, because of infirmity or age, to participate in exercise.

One study showed that convalescing patients who watched funny movies or shows, such as *The Three Stooges* or *I Love Lucy*, and spent time engaging in good, belly-shaking, tear-producing laughter, recuperated more quickly than those who did not.

The Bible tells us that "a cheerful heart is good medicine" (Proverbs 17:22), "a happy heart makes the face cheerful (Proverbs 15:13), and "the cheerful heart has a continual feast" (Proverbs 15:15).

God's Word also commands us not to conform to the way the world thinks and acts, but "be *transformed* by the renewing of your mind" (Romans 12:2).

Therein lies the key: Choose to think positive thoughts. Choose to say the encouraging word. Choose to laugh instead of get angry. Choose to look for fun. Choose joy.

"There are souls in this world which have the gift of finding joy everywhere and leaving it behind them when they go" (Frederick Faber).

And so I pray …

Lord, may I be such a soul! Amen.

MORE TEA: Read and reflect on Philippians 4:4–9.

Straight A's in Aging

For I have learned, in whatever state I am, to be content. – Philippians 4:11 NKJV

IN PREPARATION FOR AN upcoming speakers' seminar, I completed a personality profile designed to help me better understand myself and how I relate to others and react to different situations.

The strengths section was fairly easy. Determining my weaknesses, though, was a different story. None of the four choices for each of the twenty lines seemed to fit me. Many times I'd think, "I used to be this way, but I'm not anymore."

My personality type? The "perfect melancholy."

Schedule-oriented, orderly, and organized, the perfect melancholy is a detail person—persistent, thorough, accurate, and sincere. They're good with planning, explaining the facts, and keeping the records straight, but can get lost in the details and become too easily distracted and critical. I have difficulty writing tight and being concise when I speak because I think I have to include all the details and facts.

My husband, on the other hand, perfectly fits the "peaceful phlegmatic" personality type. A support person, the peaceful phlegmatic is good at staying calm and functional amid chaos, and not overreacting to a negative situation. While the perfect melancholy needs order and understanding, the peaceful phlegmatic needs rest and quiet.

Imagine someone who wants everything perfect living with someone for whom the details don't matter. The uptight living with the easygoing. I'm often running late because I've got to fold the quilt on the sofa, fluff the throw pillows, take the hanger off the bed, check the dehumidifier to see if it should be emptied, and put everything in its place. I want to walk into a perfect house when I come home.

My husband, the peaceful phlegmatic who doesn't care what the place looks like when he comes in (just have supper ready, please) and who wants to be on time for things, chastens me with a "Let it go, Michele."

Knowing my personality type has helped me to accept myself the way God created me. And recognizing my husband's personality type has given me insight into what makes him tick. You'd think, though, after being married to the man for nearly forty-six years, I'd know that already. But our marriage has lasted over four decades because we've learned to adapt—to each other and to circumstances.

This is the fourth secret to aging with grace: accepting yourself and others the way you were created and adapting to situations that come into your life, especially ones that cannot be changed.

Both Joseph and Paul found themselves in prison, not because of anything they'd done wrong but because of what they did right. To survive, they learned to accept and adapt.

"Do not be distressed and do not be angry with yourselves for selling me here, because it was to save lives that God sent me ahead of you," Joseph told his brothers when they finally caught up with each other. "So then, it was not you who sent me here, but God" (Genesis 45:5,8).

And Paul wrote from prison: "I have learned to be content whatever the circumstances … I can do everything through him who gives me strength" (Philippians 4:11,13).

The key to accepting, adapting, and learning to be content with what you hadn't planned and didn't want, is knowing that you are not the one in control. God is.

When I took the personality profile, I realized how much God had been working in my life, changing me. I hadn't thought I'd changed at all. But God used hard times, unchanging circumstances, and difficult people to change me. Iron sharpening iron. Painful but productive.

Lord, give me the serenity to accept the things I cannot change, the courage to change the things I can, and the wisdom to know the difference. Amen. (From "The Prayer of Serenity")

MORE TEA: Read and reflect on Philippians 4:11–13.

This Too Shall Pass

Be content with what you have, because God has said, "Never will I leave you; never will I forsake you." – Hebrews 13:5 NIV

THIRTY-NINE YEARS AGO, we moved from our apartment in town to what would someday be our dream home in the country, then an unfinished basement thirteen miles from town. The money we paid for rent, we reckoned, would be better spent on the house we were building ourselves.

Never did I dream it would take a more than quarter of a century to finish the project. But if I may say so myself, I was amazed I was patient for that long. With my perfectionist tendencies, living with the symphony of the hammer and saw evening after evening without playing my concerto of complaints was certainly a challenge.

At the time we moved, our oldest child was four and the baby eleven months old. Boxes, clothes, and toys cluttered every square foot as I struggled to make that concrete cubicle a home. The furnace, on loan until we could afford a new, larger one, needed repair. It was mid-November, and winter was closing in fast. A constant fire in the woodstove did little to warm up the concrete surrounding us. Insulating the place was still on our to-do list. I wore long underwear, a toboggan hat, and layers of clothing indoors.

The plumbing was still unfinished, so, for baths, we hooked up a garden hose to the water tank and fed it through a hole in the wall above the bathtub. Lugging pots of hot water from the kitchen, I flooded the bathroom floor twice.

My back ached from sleeping on an old, lumpy sofa bed mattress. Our comfortable queen-size bed was stored in the wagon shed until we made room for it.

Three days of disorganization, interruptions, and things going wrong left me struggling with my emotions.

"Why can't I have nice things the easy way like everyone else?" I grumbled. "Why am I always a 'have-not' and never a 'have'?"

My husband tried to cheer me up. "It's only temporary," he'd say.

Then, before the first week was up, an early snowstorm dumped six inches on the countryside overnight. Every two hours I bundled up even more and shoveled swirling drifts away from the only door. Flinging wet, heavy snow over my shoulder, I gave in to self-pity.

"Temporary, temporary," I fumed. "Is *everything* temporary?"

The answer came immediately: *Even if you had everything exactly the way you wanted, it would still be temporary.*

This is the fifth secret to aging with grace: Being content in your circumstances because you know that whatever your earthly condition, it's only temporary. A friend of mine is fond of saying, "This too shall pass."

Contentment is the antidote to unhappiness, envy, worry, fear, discontentment, grumbling, and bitterness.

That's not to say I don't feel envy and discontent at times. But I've learned to fight it by focusing, not on the things I can see, but on the things I can't, because "what is seen is temporary, but what is unseen is eternal" (2 Corinthians 4:18). Why get all stirred up about something that isn't going to last? I've learned that with God's help, I can make it through anything (Philippians 4:13) by fixing my eyes on what is truly permanent.

And what is permanent? God, His Word, His promises, His presence, His protection, His provision, His love, His gifts of eternal life and a home in Heaven with Him forever.

If I have God, you see, I have everything.

Lord, help me to remember that whatever my earthly condition—whether rich, poor, or in between—is only temporary. Remind me daily what's really important. Amen.

MORE TEA: Read and reflect on 2 Corinthians 4:16–18.

Treasures in Jars of Clay

So we have this treasure in jars of clay. – 2 Corinthians 4:7 NIV

WHAT EXACTLY DOES BEING beautiful entail? Wearing expensive clothes, or at least ones that don't look as though you've owned them for a lifetime? Consulting makeup and fashion experts to help you put yourself together the "right" way? Using a certain brand of hair color? Exercising every day? Having a natural beauty to your face and a body with no sags, wrinkles, or extra pouches?

Every day we're urged to be one of the "beautiful people." TV ads advise us to purchase expensive exercise equipment. Ever notice that the men and women demonstrating how easy it is to lose weight don't have to? Look at the covers of women's magazines as you stand in line at the checkout counter, and you'll see the titles of the articles inside deal with basically the same topics: "Watch those pounds melt off" (yeah, right) or "Eat all the chocolate you want and still lose weight" (in your dreams) or "Beauty Makeovers" (why does it never happen to me?).

If having an attractive, sleek body is what being beautiful is all about, how, then, can you be beautiful in your senior years, when your body is slowly, as Paul put it two millennia ago, "wasting away"? When this "jar of clay" lets you down. When your energy wanes, and you can't do as much as you used to. When reading glasses are a necessary part of your wardrobe. When you have to watch what you eat because certain foods will haunt you in the middle of the night. When every year you not only celebrate your birthday, but you also mark the breakdown of one more part of you.

Or is beauty something deeper—an inner radiance that shows on your face and in your behavior and attitude? A zest for life that can't be quenched.

People who possess this quality energize everyone they meet. You walk away smiling when the cashier looks you in the eye, gives you a hearty smile, and actually means it when she says, "Have a good day" instead of complain about how much longer she has to work. Your spirits lift when the man who bags your purchases does it with a whistle on his lips and a spring in his step.

I once knew a man who went deep-sea fishing when he was in his nineties. He lived full tilt, gardening, canning, baking bread, selling homegrown blueberries and locally produced chocolate candy. I used to tease him that he thought the speed limit was his age. But he loved people and he loved life. His body was aging, but his spirit was beautiful.

This, then, is the fifth secret to aging with grace: Enthusiasm—possessing a spirit of excitement that enables you to face each day, each thing you do, with eagerness, interest, and energy.

While we have little, if any, control over the aging process, enthusiasm is something we can cultivate. The word itself comes from a Greek word that means to be inspired and "possessed by a god." The Bible tells us to be enthusiastic all that we do: "Whatever your hand finds to do, do it with all your might" (Ecclesiastes 9:10). "Whatever you do, work at with all your heart" (Colossians 3:23).

This, then, is the key to having enthusiasm: Give yourself daily to the one and only God. His Spirit living within you gives you eternal life, inspires you, and fills you with eagerness, excitement, and energy. The Spirit of God is the treasure you carry in your jar of clay.

To age with grace, then, remember GRACE:

G – Grow

R – Rejoice

A – Accept and Adapt

C – be Content

E – have Enthusiasm.

Thank You, God, for those people I meet that brighten my day with their enthusiasm. Fill me with Your Spirit so that my excitement for living will energize and encourage those around me. Amen.

MORE TEA: Read and reflect on 2 Corinthians 4:7–5:6.

The Armor of God

Put on the whole armor of God,
that you may be able to stand against the wiles of the devil.

–Ephesians 6:11 NKJV

Not an Ornament

Stand firm, then, with the belt of truth buckled around your waist ... –Ephesians 6:14 NIV

WHEN MY FAVORITE BELT began to unravel, I tucked the frayed and broken edges into the weaving, hoping to extend its life span. Small wonder it was falling apart. I wore it every day with slacks, jeans, shorts, or a skirt. I liked the sporty look it gave my outfit for the day.

After a couple of years of daily use, however, the belt took on a worn appearance, and, in time, I could no longer hide the frayed and broken sections, no matter how hard I tried. It was time to dispose of what I'd come to depend upon to complete my daily dress.

At first I felt incomplete, but then I noticed I really didn't need the belt to hold up my bottoms. My "middle age spread" did the job just as well. All my belt had been was an ornament, something added for decoration but having no practical value.

Nearly two thousand years ago when St. Paul instructed the people of Ephesus to have the belt of truth buckled around their waists, a belt was more than an ornament. It was an important piece of a soldier's armor. A strong, wide piece worn around the middle of the body, the soldier's belt served two purposes: It protected his vital organs, and it held all the other pieces of his armor together.

In likening truth to a belt, St. Paul has shown us its importance. Truth, defined as "all that is real and will not change," is not just something we put on to make us look good. Truth has a real and vital purpose: to protect us and to hold us together. The belt of truth gives the wearer the security and peace of a clear conscience. Unlike my imitation leather belt, the belt of truth will never unravel or wear out.

Help me, O God, to bind myself with truth every day of my life. Amen.

MORE TEA: Read and reflect on Ephesians 6:10–24.

Chest Protectors

Stand firm ... with the breastplate of righteousness in place ... –Ephesians 6:14, 17 NIV

WHEN OUR BOYS WERE younger, my husband was forever reminding them of the importance of wearing the proper equipment when playing sports. So when he got his ribs bruised rough-housing with the oldest, who was in full football gear, a number of years ago, I had to bite back the "I told you so" and go and buy the biggest Ace bandage I could find. He who preached protection was sore for at least a month.

Football isn't the only activity for which participants must wear protective gear. Baseball catchers and umpires, deep sea divers, astronauts, law enforcement officials, construction workers, firefighters, and soldiers all wear specially designed equipment to protect their bodies from serious injury. Especially vulnerable is the torso, where our vital organs are located. Of utmost importance is the heart, which keeps us alive by pumping oxygen and nutrient-rich blood throughout our bodies to every organ we need to live. That's why chest protectors are so important.

In spiritual warfare, we also need a chest protector. St. Paul calls it the “breastplate of righteousness.” Righteousness is, most simply, right thinking, right feeling, and right living. When the winds of trial threaten my faith, when anger over a careless remark or action rises unbidden, when low funds tempt me to delay paying what I owe, when desire for others’ respect becomes more important than truth and honesty, then I need to bind that chest protector around me even more tightly. I should never, ever be without it. I’m much too vulnerable to the enemy’s attacks. Only with it secured and in place can I stand firm.

Only with the righteousness You give through Your death and resurrection, Lord Jesus, can I stand firm in the battles I face every day. Thank You. Amen.

MORE TEA: Read and reflect on Romans 3:21–26.

The Right Shoes

Stand firm ... having shod your feet with the equipment of the gospel of peace. –Ephesians 6:14, 15 RSV

GROWING UP, MY SON David took the shoe trophy for the Huey household. He had a pair of shoes for every occasion and activity, it seemed: baseball, basketball, skateboarding, school, play, work, fishing, and hunting. It would have been so such simpler—and cheaper—if only one pair would do.

Each type of shoe, however, had a different job to do and was made accordingly. David's baseball shoes were equipped with spikes, which gave him traction as he raced around the bases or through the grassy outfield. His basketball shoes provided the ankle and arch support he needed as he sprinted and jumped on a hard, wooden floor. Sturdy work boots, like hunting boots, gave him support and protection as he tramped over the uneven terrain of the woods in search of firewood or game. The shoes he wore for fishing were made to keep his feet dry, while the boots he pulled on for hunting were insulated to keep them warm. If his feet hurt—or were cold and wet—it was hard for him to concentrate on the job he had to do. The right shoe enabled him to do the job right.

Just as David needed the proper footwear whatever he did, so I need the right "shoes" for the job God has given me—to take the peace He offers through His Son Jesus to the world around me (John 14:27, Matthew 28:20, Acts 1:8).

Before I can bring peace to others, however, I need to have peace with God through His Son. Only then do I have the traction, support, warmth, and protection I need to run life's bases or stand my ground against the enemy.

Only when I have God's Son in my heart do I have the right shoes on my feet.

"How beautiful on the mountains are the feet of those who bring good news, who proclaim peace ..." (Isaiah 52:7 NIV) Lord, let my feet be beautiful!

MORE TEA: Read and reflect on Ephesians 6:10–20.

When Arrows Come Flyin'

Take up the shield of faith, with which you can extinguish all the flaming arrows of the evil one. –Ephesians 6:16 NIV

"NEVER MAKE PLANS," A friend once advised me. "Take it only one day at a time."

That's wise advice, considering some days so much comes flying at me that I'd like to go hide all by myself for awhile. A week would do nicely.

The expected things I can handle. It's the unexpected, unplanned, unforeseen things that throw my crammed schedule out of whack and trip me up, like getting sick.

Since I spend the weekdays working on various writing projects, Saturday is really the only full day I have scheduled for such pleasantries as laundry and house cleaning. One Saturday, however, I woke up with a sore throat and sinus congestion, so I took a twelve-hour cold pill, thinking it would get me through the day. I was wrong. All it did was make me drowsy. I snoozed all afternoon and evening, while my work went undone.

Since Sunday is my day of rest, my Saturday chores were still staring at me on Monday morning. Monday morning, however, I was still sick. Tuesday I called the doctor for antibiotics, but that bug hung on for three weeks. It wasn't the congestion but the fatigue that kept me on the couch, staring at the dust and disorder that got worse every day.

It's when things pile up and I feel my schedule slipping out of control that I find I'm more susceptible to temptation. Ditto when I'm tired or sick. Most often I get down on myself and feel like a failure. Then it's easy to cave in and feel sorry for myself. Self-pity makes me testy, and I before I know it, I'm snapping at my husband. Then the guilt sets in.

I need to learn to use my shield of faith more by remembering Who is really in control of the events of my life, even getting sick. Sometimes those are the only times God can get my attention—when I'm flat on my back and helpless. I'm more willing to listen then and more apt to learn that it is God's faithfulness and not my own weak faith that helps me to cope when arrows come flying.

Great is Your faithfulness, Lord, unto me. Thank You. Amen.

MORE TEA: Read and reflect on Ephesians 6:10–18.

Stinkin' Thinkin'

Take the helmet of salvation ... –Ephesians 6:17 RSV

WHEN MY TWO OLDEST children were in grade school, I hosted and taught a Bible club in my home once a week. More than thirty kids hiked across the field after school and kicked off their muddy shoes or snowy boots on the floor I'd just cleaned. Dropping their backpacks and coats, they trooped into the living room, cookies and Kool-Aid in hand, and plopped down on the carpet.

Most of the time I convinced myself the clutter didn't matter—that there were eternal rewards for my efforts. But one time I let the mess get to me.

After the crowd left, I sent my children upstairs to begin their homework while I started supper and cleaned up. I wasn't seeing the eternal rewards right then, only the mud, puddles, crumbs, and other residue left from a house-full of hungry, hopping kids.

Are they even getting anything from the Bible lessons? I wondered, hurling my sweeper over the floor for the second time that day. *Should I even bother?*

The more I thought, the madder I got. When my oldest son came downstairs to ask me something, I snapped at him, letting loose a few words I thought I'd eliminated from my vocabulary.

"Mom," he said, looking me straight in the eye, "Look at what Satan is doing to you."

I stopped in mid-sweep. He was right. I was guilty of stinkin' thinkin'. And those thoughts, set loose in my mind, slithered into my heart and poisoned the way I felt and, consequently, the way I acted.

Stinkin' thinkin' is sin, no matter how we try to justify it. And sin is not a popular word in today's feel-good society where everyone, it seems, is a victim of something or other. We do wrong things, we're told, not because we were born with selfish, rebellious hearts, as the Bible teaches, but because we are reacting to something someone did along the way to hurt us or to life's unfairness.

But sin is our whole problem. It is the seed, the root, the trunk, the branches, the rotten fruit. It is the Pandora's box that separates us from a loving and holy God, and it must be routed if we are to become the persons God created us to be.

I yanked sin's roots when I believed that Jesus died to save me from the penalty and power of sin, and invited Him to take control of my life. I've learned to put on my helmet of salvation and choose to think only about those things that are true, right, pure, lovely, admirable, excellent, and praiseworthy (Philippians 4:8). This helmet protects my mind while the Holy Spirit transforms and renews it (Romans 12:2).

"The mind of sinful man is death," St. Paul wrote, "but the mind controlled by the Spirit is life and peace" (Romans 8:6).

Isn't that what we seek? The Bible tells us that God will "keep him in perfect peace whose mind is stayed" on Him (Isaiah 26:3). The result of keeping our thoughts on God—and all He is—is peace, which, in turn, will guard, or keep, our thoughts and emotions (Philippians 4:6), and, consequently, our actions.

And that beats stinkin' thinkin' anytime.

Dear God, help me to choose to think the right thoughts, even when everything seems to be going wrong. Amen.

MORE TEA: Read and reflect on Ephesians 6:10–18.

Virus Protection

Take ... the sword of the Spirit, which is the Word of God ...
–Ephesians 6:17 RSV

THE WINDOW POPPED UP on my computer screen as I booted up my system for the day's work session.

"Oh no," I groaned. "Not again." The notice informed me that I needed to update my virus protection files.

When I first bought my computer, I pooh-poohed the idea of purchasing a program to protect my system from viruses, nasty programs that sick people write and send through the Internet that either make your computer act wacky or shut it down completely.

I got through a year without incident. Then someone informed me that I'd sent an email that had a virus attached. I didn't even know I was sick. All the horror stories I'd heard about virus-caused computer crashes, I realized, could happen to me. So I bought an anti-virus program and installed it.

I lost count of the times the program arrested an incoming virus and jailed it in quarantine. Since I don't like the idea of anything potentially harmful in my system, even though it's disabled in a safe place, I'd mutter a prayer that I didn't mess things up, hold my breath, and click on the DELETE button. So far I'm still in business.

Screening emails for incoming viruses isn't the only way the anti-virus program protects my computer. Once a week, it automatically scans my complete system for hidden viruses.

Simply installing the program and letting it do its job, however, still isn't enough.

I need to update it regularly by adding new information so the program can identify the latest viruses going around and disarm them before they have a chance to wreak their havoc.

I have an anti-virus program for my spirit, too. It's called the Word of God. I update it each time I read, study, and memorize Scripture (Psalm 119:11). It abides there, deep in my heart, mind, and soul, protecting me from any incoming things that could harm me. These viruses, once attached to my spirit, either make me "act wacky" until I determine to delete the sin from my life, or control me so that I don't do what God wants me to do.

A "window" pops up whenever I need to be reminded that God will give me the strength to resist temptation (1 Corinthians 10:13), that trials perfect and strengthen my faith (1 Peter 1:6,7; James 1:2-4), that tribulations are the lot of life (John 16:33), and that I can be forgiven when I fail (1 John 1:9). Reading the Bible regularly "scans" my heart, mind, and soul for any hidden sins lurking there.

"The word of God is living and active. Sharper than any double-edged sword, it penetrates even to dividing soul and spirit, joints and marrow; it judges the thoughts and attitudes of the heart" (Hebrews 4:12 NIV).

Taking the time each day to read the Bible helps me not only to identify sin when it tries to attach itself to me, but also to boot it out. And that's protection I wouldn't want to do without.

"Search me, O God, and know my heart; test me and know my anxious thoughts. See if there is any offensive way in me, and lead me in the way everlasting." (Psalm 139:23–24 NIV)

MORE TEA: Read and reflect on Ephesians 6:1–18.

The Beatitudes

Blessed are you ...

–Matthew 5:11 NKJV

Feeling the Need

Blessed are the poor in spirit, for theirs is the kingdom of heaven. – Matthew 5:3 NIV

WHEN I WAS ABOUT ten years old, my father was laid off from his job at the steel mill. In the years that followed, we learned the difference between *want* and *need*. I remember when I was in high school and went to a fast food restaurant after practice with a carload of majorettes and not ordering anything. "I'm not hungry," I'd say. But I was.

At home meatless meals were the standard fare, and a roll of toilet paper took the place of a box of tissues.

"What's this?" my sister's boyfriend wisecracked when he spied the roll on top of a kitchen cabinet. "Johnson's Poverty Program?"

In today's world, poverty is seen as a negative. What does it mean to be poor? It means you don't have the income to provide adequately the necessities of life: food, clothing, and shelter.

That's why it's hard to understand what Jesus meant when He said that the poor in spirit are blessed. Poverty and blessings usually don't go together. When you're poor, you don't feel blessed. When you're poor, feel your neediness, your hunger, your thirst, your want for better things. Hopelessness and despair worm their way into your heart and mind, and devour your dreams. You battle envy, embarrassment, and shame.

So what exactly did Jesus mean when He said, "Blessed are the poor in spirit, for theirs is the kingdom of heaven"?

Perhaps it has to do with that little word, *need.*

God doesn't condemn being poor. Throughout His Word, He commands us to look after those who are in need (Matthew 25:31–46), to help them, not mistreat them.

He does, however, caution against trusting in riches. "Do not store up for yourselves treasures on earth, where moth and rust destroy, and where thieves break in and steal … No one can serve two masters … You cannot serve both God and money" (Matthew 6:19–24).

So does that mean He wants us to be poor? In a sense, yes.

Through the Apostle John, He told the wealthy Laodicean church that they were really poor: "You say, 'I am rich. I have everything I want. I don't need a thing!' And you don't realize that you are wretched and miserable and poor and blind and naked. I advise you to buy gold from me—gold that has been purified by fire. Then you will be rich" (Revelation 3:17–18).

Starving people reach a point where they no longer feel hunger, where they no longer feel the need for food. These Laodicieans were starving spiritually, but they had reached the point where they no longer felt their need for spiritual food. Material riches were the empty fillers that deadened their spiritual hunger. They did not feel the need for anything, neither material nor spiritual. They were spiritually poor, and they didn't even know it.

"Blessed are the poor in spirit who feel and understand their need," Jesus is saying in Matthew 5:3. They are blessed because they aren't trusting in material riches, they aren't puffed up with spiritual pride, thinking involvement in kingdom affairs and tithing and giving to the needy are sufficient.

They are blessed because they feel a constant need for God Himself. As a deer pants for streams of water, so their souls long for God (Psalm 42:1). They understand that "in him (God) we live and move and have our being" (Acts 17:28).

They hunger and thirst after Him. They long for a personal relationship with Him through His Son. They hunger after His Word and thirst for time with Him. They understand their need—and it is for God only.

Dear God, sometimes I ease my spiritual hunger with empty fillers, such as my Christian activities, instead of the spiritual food that comes from seeking You alone. Forgive me. Amen.

MORE TEA: Read and reflect on Revelation 4:17–18.

A Time to Weep

Blessed are those who mourn, for they shall be comforted. – Matthew 5:4 NIV

I EXPERIENCED GRIEF FOR the first time when my father died. I was twenty years old and in college. I learned firsthand what personal loss meant. There were no grief counselors to walk me through the long nights. I had to step into the future without the man who was my hero.

Following my father's death, my mother's health declined. Until her death, Alzheimer's disease robbed me of the mother I needed more now that I had children of my own. I'd stand at the card racks every Mother's Day and weep. I grieved my mother for the fifteen years I slowly lost her. When she died, I was comforted, for her spirit—her vibrant personality and generous love—finally soared free.

My beloved Aunt Betty passed away in 2003. It was to her, my godmother, my idol, that I dedicated my first book. From the time I took my first breath, she was a golden ray of sunshine, warming, welcoming, loving me as I was, guiding and encouraging me to become what she knew I could be.

Then, four months later, my sister was suddenly taken from us. She and I were supposed to commiserate growing old together. Instead I sat on the love seat, shivering, trembling, sobbing, for days. I reread her last email over and over until my computer crashed and I lost those priceless last words.

We grieve when we lose something precious to us. We mourn because what we lost can never be replaced. There is a void in our lives, a hole in our hearts, that nothing can fill. But we learn to go on.

This is the kind of grief God wants us to feel for sin—our own, personal sin and the sin in the world around us. This is the mourning Jesus meant when He said, "Blessed are those who mourn, for they shall be comforted."

Why are we to mourn sin? Because sin has robbed us of something precious and vital—a relationship with a holy God who created us for Himself. Without God, there is a hole in our spiritual hearts, a void in our lives nothing but He can fill. We try to go on but something is missing.

The first three chapters of Genesis tell the whole sad story. Ever since then, man has been running from the One who hasn't given up on him. With our sin, we cannot stand in His holy presence (Isaiah 6:1–7). We cannot remove our sin ourselves. Only the blood of a perfect substitute for us can do that. And God sent His own Son to be that substitute. When Jesus died on that cross, He took my punishment (Romans 6:23). His shed blood removes my sin so that I can enter God's presence (1 John 1:9; 5:11–12) and spend eternity there. But we have to accept His gift. Some don't.

The Greek word for "blessed" in these verses (*makarioi*) is an adjective that means happy. How can we be happy and sad at the same time?

We can be sad for the sin that creates a barrier between us and the God who wants us with Him forever, and we can be happy for the way He has provided for us to His home in Heaven.

But we aren't to keep this good news to ourselves. We are to feel grief at the sin in the world around us so deeply that we are to mourn, and our mourning will drive us to spread the Word.

When you mourn, the nights are long. But mourning is over when the Son rises. And then His rays will warm, welcome, love, guide, and encourage you until that day you finally arrive home.

Father, I don't mourn enough. Give me a heart for the hurting, a love for the lost, and a sorrow for the sin in the world around me. Open my eyes to the opportunities to tell others of Your love. Amen.

MORE TEA: Read and reflect on Ezekiel 9:1–6 and Psalm 51.

Meek Is Macho

Blessed are the meek, for they will inherit the earth. – Matthew 5:5 NIV

A. W. TOZER ONCE SAID that if you take the Beatitudes and turn them wrong side out, you have a pretty good picture of the human race. We humans tend to nurture the exact opposite of the traits Jesus defined as characteristics of His followers.

Take meekness, for instance. You don't have to look far to see that we as a society do not look upon this godly characteristic with favor. The attitude of pop culture is, if you're meek, you're weak. Our heroes are the Rambo-type tough guys, the macho men who are strong, smart, rich, witty, and suave. The meek guy is the sissy, the wimp, the nerd, the comic character we laugh at.

Yet Jesus said that the meek, not the macho, are the ones who are blessed, who are truly happy. (The word used, *makarioi*, translates "happy.")

Look up "meekness" in a dictionary, and you get anything from "weak, unassuming, servile, and timid" to "peaceful, gentle, humble, and patient."

God's Word, however, defines meekness not with words but with examples. Abraham, Moses, David, Paul, and Jesus Himself, are all examples of meekness, which I have come to define as "power and strength under control."

Abraham, to whom God promised land as far as his eye could see, didn't lord his relationship with the Creator over his nephew Lot, but rather allowed the immature, grasping, greedy, selfish younger man to chose the best part of the land. Moses, who confronted the most powerful man on earth, led a nation of stubborn, whining people out of slavery and across a Mid-Eastern desert (with Pharoah's army hot on their heels at one point), was "very meek, more than all men that were on the face of the earth" (Numbers 12:3).

David, God's man who was promised the throne of Israel, had more than one chance to kill his enemy King Saul but refused, allowing God determine the course of events (1 Samuel 24, 26). And when he was on the run from his throne-usurping son, he refused to retaliate when cursed (2 Samuel 16:9–12).

Paul, who was responsible for practically single-handedly spreading Christianity in the first century world, was another example of meekness. In spite of the beatings, floggings, stonings, shipwrecks, and imprisonments (2 Corinthians 11:23–30), in spite of being chased from town to town by his enemies, he still persevered in his mission, and encouraged others to "always give yourselves fully to the work of the Lord, because you know that your labor in the Lord is not in vain" (1 Corinthians 15:58).

And Jesus Himself is the prime example of meekness: "Come to me, all you who are weary and heavy laden," He says. "For I am meek and lowly in heart, and you will find rest for your souls" (Matthew 11:28–30).

So what does this mean for me today? It means not retaliating, in word or deed; accepting what is out of my control and making the best of it, believing that God is in control (Romans 8:28). It means I'm not a braggart or showy person, grasping the best for myself. It means I shut up when provoked because it takes more strength to walk away that to fight back. It means I take God at His word and practice meekness with a conscious effort, because it is not a natural trait.

In *The Pursuit of God*, Tozer wrote, "The meek man is not a human mouse afflicted with a sense of his own inferiority. Rather he may be in his moral life as bold as a lion and as strong as Samson; but he has stopped being fooled about himself. He has accepted God's estimate of his own life. He knows he is as weak and helpless as God declared him to be, but paradoxically, he knows at the same time that he is in the sight of God of more importance than angels. In himself, nothing; in God, everything. That is his motto."

If you think meekness is weakness, try being meek for a week.

Dear God, help me to be meek. Amen.

MORE TEA: Read and reflect on Genesis 13.

Danger: Apathy at Work

Blessed are those who hunger and thirst for righteousness, for they will be filled. –Matthew 5:6 NIV

IT MUST HAVE BEEN quite a scene. If there had been newspapers in the first century, the headlines would have announced: "Prophet From Nazareth Goes Berserk: Merchants Clean Up After Miracle Man Trashes Temple Courts."

It's hard to imagine gentle Jesus—the One who, on trial for His life, said not a word in His own defense; who healed, consoled, and preached peaceful living—brandishing a handmade whip, driving out cattle and sheep, overturning tables, and flinging coins in anger. Temper tantrum? Hardly. Jesus Himself gave the reason for His actions: "It is written, 'My house will be a house of prayer,' but you have made it 'a den of robbers'" (Luke 19:46).

The apostle John adds to the account: "His disciples remembered that it is written, 'Zeal for your house will consume me'" (John 2:17).

On another occasion, the Son of God delivered a scathing chastisement to the Pharisees for their hardened hearts and hypocritical lifestyle, and for preventing people from believing in Him and entering the kingdom of Heaven (Matthew 23:1–39). Few instances of Jesus' anger are recorded in the Gospels, but each time His anger was for a just cause.

While the Bible warns us against the dangers of harboring anger and allowing it to control us, we should get angry when we see the innocent suffer because of the guilty. Righteous anger—anger for a just cause—differs from selfish anger, which is anger born of thinking only of ourselves and wanting our own way.

Righteous anger spurs us into action. Corruption spurred Martin Luther to nail his Ninety-five Theses to a German church door. Prejudice spurred Martin Luther King to dream of a society in which all people of every race and color would enjoy the same privileges and respect given to the whites. Spiritual apathy spurred Jonathan Edwards to pen his famous sermon, "Sinners in the Hands of an Angry God" and John Wesley to launch a spiritual revival in eighteenth century England.

In our day and age, outrage against euthanasia and a belief in the sanctity of life spurred an outcry against removing Terry Schiavo's feeding tubes.

Look around. Declining moral standards and spiritual apathy abound. Greed, corruption, and selfishness run rampant. Prime time television spews filth that corrupts the minds of small children. Blatant profanity and lewdness lace the lyrics of popular music. It's okay to use God's name in vain in public, but don't you dare pray in public. It's okay to wear T-shirts and display bumper stickers that offend others with obscenities, but you'd better cover up the Ten Commandments.

Schools are closing because of declining enrollment. The Social Security system is in danger because there are fewer workers in the work force to support the retiring baby boomers. Yet in 1973, the Supreme Court said it was okay to take the lives of unborn children. If those babies had been allowed to be born, would we have the crises we have today?

This is nothing new. The writer of Judges noted that "every man did that which was right in his own eyes" (Judges 21:25). What Isaiah wrote centuries ago still applies to us today: "We all, like sheep, have gone astray, each one of us has turned to his own way" (Isaiah 53:6).

There's a story about a young man who traveled a far and dangerous route to ask a sage, reputed to be the wisest man on earth, how he could attain such wisdom. He found the sage, who led the young man to a stream then held his head under the running water until the young man, after a struggle, broke free.

"Why did you do that?" the young man gasped. "All I wanted to know was how to become as wise as you!"

"When you desire wisdom as much as you needed that breath of air," the sage replied, "you'll find it."

When we want righteousness as much as we need the next breath, we, too, will allow righteous anger to spur us to speak out against the wrongs around us and point the way to the only hope we have: God.

Place in me a righteous anger, O God, so that it will spur me to make a difference for You in my world. Amen.

MORE TEA: Read and reflect on John 2:13–17.

Surprise Party

Blessed are the merciful, for they will be shown mercy. – Matthew 5:7 NIV

WHEN I WAS IN grade school, I always wanted to have a real birthday party—you know, when you invite the whole class at school. Every year when I asked, though, my mother's answer was always the same: "No." Maybe the class size of nearly fifty had something to do with it.

"Please, Mom," I'd plead. "Everyone else has one. Why do I always have to be different?"

No amount of begging, whining, or pouting, however, changed her mind. Her lopsided cakes were for family only.

One year, though, I was determined to have the kind of party I wanted, in spite of my mother's usual "no." So I invited all the kids in my third grade class to come to my house on Saturday, November 5, for my birthday party. My mother, of course, knew nothing about it.

I bowled in a youth bowling league on Saturday mornings, and when I left the house that day, I still hadn't told my mother about the party. The walk home after bowling was the longest walk I ever took in my life! I trudged the eight blocks home in the cold, damp November wind, thinking of how much trouble I was going to be in once the kids started showing up at my door.

Not only was I going to be in the dog house at home, but I'd be the laughing stock of the whole school once word got out about the party with a lopsided cake, and not enough ice cream and pop. Don't even mention games. That was not my mother's forte.

When I stepped into the dining room a few minutes before two—the time I told everyone to come—I gasped in surprise. There in the middle of the table, set for a party, was a big, decorated birthday cake!

"How did you find out?" I blurted to my mother.

"Vivian's mother called to ask me what time your party started," she said.

I breathed a sigh of relief. *Thank you, Mrs. Bludis.*

"We'll talk about this after the party," my mother said quietly as someone knocked. "Go answer the door."

For the next three hours, I tried to ignore the sick feeling in the pit of my stomach. I'd probably be grounded for the rest of my life. When the last guest left, I hurried to help clean up, grateful to my mom for helping me save face and hoping my initiative would lessen my punishment.

"What would you have done if Mrs. Bludis hadn't called?" my mother asked me after we were done.

I shrugged.

"I didn't understand how important this was to you. I'm sorry," Mom said, "but I hope you realize you were wrong to go behind my back."

I nodded.

As it turned out, my only punishment was three agonizing hours imagining what my just desserts would be when I could have been enjoying my birthday party.

My mother taught me an important lesson in mercy that day. While it isn't easy to forgive someone who has done something wrong, showing undeserved kindness blesses both the giver and the receiver, and brings healing to broken relationships.

I deserved justice. Instead I received a birthday present I never forgot.

Thank you, God, that Your mercies are new every morning. I sure need them everyday. Amen.

MORE TEA: Read and reflect on Matthew 18:21–35.

Sinner Saved by Grace

Blessed are the pure in heart, for they will see God. – Matthew 5:8 NIV

JUST CALL ME "Messy Michele." Not that I live in disorder and clutter, because I cannot function well, if at all, if my immediate environs are disorganized. It's because I rarely can eat or drink anything without spilling or splattering something on me.

I can don a white sweater before I leave the house, but by the time I arrive at my destination, you can bet that coffee stains have added themselves to the design. One time I took spaghetti for lunch to heat in the microwave at school. Of course, that morning, without thinking of what I'd planned for lunch, I put on a white blouse.

But I was careful. I covered the front of my blouse with two or three paper towels, held the dish next to my mouth and gingerly forked in small portions. I thought I'd emerged unscathed until I looked in the mirror. There, on the shoulder of my white blouse, was a small red splotch of spaghetti sauce!

It's hopeless. No matter how careful I try to be, somehow I attract the splotches, splatters, and spills like a magnet attracts iron. I've learned to carry a roll of paper towels in my vehicle and keep a stain removal chart in the laundry room, along with a half-gallon jug and a bottle of liquid stain remover.

Even with all the laundry boosters, though, some stains don't come out. But I've found that if I hang the laundered-but-still-stained garment on the line outside on a sunny day, the sun's rays will bleach out the stain.

So it is with my spirit. I cannot emerge from living in this world unscathed by the sin that surrounds me daily. Most days I struggle with my humanness, and I fail to live up to my Lord's command to be perfect and pure (Matthew 5:48, 1 Timothy 5:22).

I can't be a saint. I'm too much of a sinner. I face the quandary St. Paul found himself in: "It seems a fact of life that when I want to do what is right, I inevitably do what is wrong. I love God's law with all my heart. But there is another law at work within me that is at war with my mind. This law wins the fight and makes me a slave to the sin still within me. Oh, what a miserable person I am! Who will free me from this life that is dominated by sin?" (Romans 7:21–24)

How can God expect us as Christians to be perfect and pure? When our spirits are so willing, and our flesh is so weak? How can He expect sinners to be saints?

Perhaps the key is understanding what a saint really is. In many of his letters to the churches, Paul called the believers "saints." Not sinners. In Romans 1:7, Paul addressed the letter "to all in Rome who are loved by God and are *called* to be saints." We are called to be saints, to live pure, perfect, holy lives.

Impossible? Yes, if we try to do it in our own human power. But there is a supernatural power available to live holy lives: God's Holy Spirit. We allow ourselves to be controlled not by our sinful, human nature, with which we war every day, but by the Holy Spirit, who indwells every believer at the moment of salvation (Romans 8:5–11).

Why, then, if I have the Holy Spirit living in me, do I still fail? Because my human nature, although no longer in control, still resides within me. Personal holiness is not instantaneous. It's a lifetime process, acquired through many failures, trials, tribulations, and sorrows; watered with both storms and showers of human tears; and cleansed by the rays of the Son.

While I live on this earth, in this "body of death," as Paul called it (Romans 7:24), I am going to fail. But, praise God, "there is now no condemnation for those who belong to Christ Jesus." While I stand at the foot of Calvary's cross, where the Son's rays bleach out my sin-stain, God sees not Michele the sinner, but Michele the saint.

That's what a saint really is: a sinner—saved by grace!

Thank You, Father, for giving me what I need to live a life pleasing to You. Amen.

MORE TEA: Read and reflect on Romans 7:7–8:17.

Peacemaker? Or Peace-Breaker?

Blessed are the peacemakers, for they will be called sons of God. –Matthew 5:9 NIV

SO FAR I'M ZERO-FOR-TWO—with the airlines, that is. One year I had to cut my trip short by a week because my baggage was destined for Pittsburgh, not Charleston, SC, where I was to meet my daughter and her family for a couple days at the beach. But that confusion was my fault. I hadn't canceled my Pittsburgh flight when I booked the Charleston one.

The next time it wasn't my fault. I packed carefully for a three-week trip, two weeks at my daughter's in South Carolina, then a week at a writers' conference near Pittsburgh. After a brief layover at Washington Dulles airport, I arrived at the Columbia, SC, airport and waited at the baggage claim for at least five minutes after everyone else from my flight left. My book bag had come through, but the suitcase with all my clothes had not.

When I filed a missed baggage claim, I was told that my suitcase was still at the Washington Dulles airport and that it would be on the next flight to Columbia, which would arrive at

7 p.m., five hours away. The agent at the baggage claim desk assured me the airline would deliver it to my daughter's that evening.

Around 9 p.m. we called the toll-free number the agent had given me, and an automated voice informed us that my luggage would be delivered between 8 p.m. and midnight. It wasn't. My daughter and son-in-law stayed up until after midnight, making additional calls, two of which somehow got disconnected, and the third for which they waited on hold for forty-five minutes before hanging up.

When my suitcase hadn't arrived by 9 a.m. the next day, we called again, this time actually getting to talk to a real, live human being, who, after giving us the same runaround we got the night before, told us it would arrive by noon. It didn't.

Around 4 p.m., I called the baggage claim number again, and when I was put on hold to wait for a customer representative, the connection was broken. Considering I had to suffer through the whole exhaustive menu thing just to get to that point, I was beginning to get just a little irritated, which, of course, is an understatement.

Since I wasn't getting anywhere with the baggage claim department, I punched in the number for Customer Relations and learned that "customer relations" is the term the airline uses for the person who tells the caller to calm down, asks for important information such as your name and phone number, listens to your complaint, then tells you she can't do anything to help you. And if you're not satisfied with her answers and ask to talk to her supervisor, she refuses.

"So what good are you if you can't help solve the problem?" I practically shouted, hanging up.

Fighting to rein in my temper, I called baggage claim again, and this time was told that my luggage was en route and I would have it "within the hour." I didn't.

I finally got it shortly after 7 p.m., with a golden "Cleared" seal of the Department of Homeland Security.

I could justify my anger: My luggage was intentionally delayed; I was ignored, lied to, and given the runaround. I felt helpless and at the mercy of giant corporation to whom I was unimportant.

But, as a Christian, I cannot justify my behavior. "If it is possible, as far as it depends on you, live at peace with everyone," God's Word commands us in Romans 12:18. It was possible. My temper depends on me. But I chose to be a peace-breaker, not a peacemaker.

Father, forgive me for acting in a way that brings shame to Your Holy Name. Remind me that I am Your Child, and help to behave accordingly. Amen.

MORE TEA: Read and reflect on James 3:17–18

Boundaries and Balance

For everything there is a season ...

–Ecclesiastes 3:1 NKJV

Why Boundaries?

In the beginning God created the heavens and the earth. – Genesis 1:1 NIV

IN ROBERT FROST'S POEM "Mending Wall," two neighbors take a springtime walk along the wall dividing their property, replacing stones and rebuilding the wall after the winter.

I understand why they had to do this. Our house is situated on a hillside, and landscaping the sloped yard presented a bit of a challenge. So my husband built a stone wall in the yard below the house to hold back the soil and keep it from moving. Every spring, though, after a winter of the ground freezing and thawing, expanding and contracting, my husband has to replace the stones that have shifted or fallen off completely.

In our case, the wall doesn't mark a boundary, but serves to beautify the property and, more importantly, to retain the soil to keep it from shifting and eroding.

The fence around our garden, however, is anything but aesthetic—especially when I tie plastic grocery bags on the thin, flexible wire to scare away the country critters. In this case, the boundary serves to keep the unwanted out.

My neighbors have fences, too—electrified boundaries to keep their horses and cows in the pastures designated for them. “Good fences make good neighbors,” Frost wrote. I agree. I don’t want my neighbors’ horses and cows wandering in my yard, even though the fertilizer they’d leave behind could be used on the garden.

Walls, fences, and boundaries serve different purposes: to hold back, retain, keep the unwanted out and the wanted in, mark property lines, and in some cases, beautify. In order to have order and not chaos, we need to establish and maintain boundaries.

Take creation, for instance. At first the earth was “a shapeless, chaotic mass” (Genesis 1:2 TLB). Then God established boundaries: He separated the light (day) from the darkness (night), the water from the sky, the seas from the dry land. The first man and woman were given a boundary, too—not to eat of a certain tree. And when they did (Frost also wrote, “Something there is that doesn’t love a wall.”), a boundary was placed around Eden (see Genesis 3:24).

When God gave His people, the Israelites, boundaries in the form of the Ten Commandments, He wanted to protect them, not hinder or hurt them. But once again, Frost’s observation, “Something there is that doesn’t love a wall” came into play.

Boundaries are a vital part of society. Without them, everyone would do what’s right in their own eyes (see Judges 21:25), and chaos would reign.

A life without boundaries, then, is not a life of freedom, a life to do what you want when you want, how you want, and how long you want. Pull out all the stops and what do you have? Chaos, catastrophe, destruction, disaster.

Just look at wildfires. Fire contained brings us warmth, gives us cooked food, and relaxes us. But fire uncontained produces destruction.

Look at the devastation caused by flooding. Water within its bounds provides us with transportation, nourishment, energy, and pleasure.

Look at an area after a hurricane blasts through. Wind within a certain range gives us refreshing breezes, energy, electricity. Wind unrestrained results in disaster.

In her Bible study *Breathe* Priscilla Shirer states, "Boundaries are not burdens. They are gifts."

Think about the boundaries in your life. What are they? What purposes do they serve? Do they hinder or help? Are they burdens or gifts?

Open my mind, heart, and spirit, O Lord, to what You want to reveal to me about the boundaries in my life. Amen.

MORE TEA: Read and reflect on Genesis 1–3.

Sabbath Margins

"The Sabbath was made for man, not man for the Sabbath." –Jesus, as quoted in Mark 2:27 NIV

WHAT IMAGE COMES TO mind when you hear the word *Sabbath*?

A day of rest and relaxation? A day to restore spent batteries? A day to finally schedule those fun activities you don't have time for the rest of the week? A day to worship God? A nice, long, delicious Sunday afternoon nap? Parking it before the television to watch the game? Or a day to catch up with all the work you couldn't fit into Monday through Saturday?

For me, Sabbath meant a day of rest, and that, traditionally, was Sunday. And only Sunday.

So when I read Priscilla Shirer's view of Sabbath in her Bible study *Breathe*, her words stopped me in my Sabbath tracks: "God always and eternally intended Sabbath to be a *lifestyle*—an attitude, a perspective, an orientation for living that enables us to govern our lives and steer clear of bondage." (emphasis mine)

What bondage? I live in a free country. That makes me free, right?

Wrong. There are many things that can enslave me.

Like to-do lists. I cram too many "must-do" items in my daily schedule then feel like a big, fat failure when I don't accomplish everything on the list.

"How can I get everything done on my to-do list?" I once lamented.

"Put less on your list," someone answered.

I wish I would've heeded that advice when it was given to me. Instead I developed a daily and weekly schedule on my computer using an Excel spreadsheet. To which I am a slave.

Oh, I get such pleasure in crossing items off! So much so that I'll remember something that needs done that isn't on the list, do it, then add it to the list so I can cross it off. That's pretty pathetic.

We become dependent on that to which we are addicted. I depended on crossing off items on the list to make me feel good about myself, to feel productive, perhaps to give my life meaning. But all I was doing was spinning my wheels and burning myself out. No wonder I felt overwhelmed, plumbed out, ready to quit the ministries to which God called me.

I needed rest, but, more important, I needed to examine my unrealistic lists and schedules and determine, prayerfully, what to cut and what to keep.

And I needed to set what Priscilla calls Sabbath margins around what remained—establish boundaries so I can have time for *Shabbat*. Boundaries, remember, aren't burdens, but gifts.

Shabbat comes from a Hebrew word that means to cease, to stop, to rest—verbs that require decisive action.

God created Sabbath on the seventh day to give the rest of what He created balance. A life without Sabbath, without rest, is out of balance. Sabbath is not an option but an integral part of life. A lifestyle, not a day.

I'm still wrapping my mind around Sabbath being a lifestyle.

As I examine my schedule and place margins around those activities I choose to keep, I'm beginning to understand that Sabbath is not just Sunday but every day of the week.

Where do you need to put Sabbath margins?

Father, I pray for guidance, wisdom and discernment as I continue to follow Your lead of establishing Sabbath margins in my life so that nothing holds me captive but You. Amen.

MORE TEA:

Read and reflect on Genesis 2:1–3 and Exodus 20:8–11.

Just Say No

"Just say a simple, 'Yes, I will,' or 'No, I won't.'" –Jesus, as quoted in Matthew 5:37 NLT

I SHOULD HAVE JUST said no.

But how does a mother say no to a grown son who asks her to doggie-sit his year-old Australian Shepherd for a week?

Tucker, the aforementioned Aussie, is the most hyperactive dog on the planet. Although he's calmed down some and our son has worked with him, he's still a pup with more energy than he knows to do with. Except race around the house every evening and chew everything in sight.

Okay, that's an exaggeration. Not everything. Just a fake apple from a basket for decoration, my *National Geographic* bird book, one of my SmartWool merino hiking socks (my favorite pair), the charging cord for my phone, the cap for my stainless steel water bottle, and whatever paper, plastic, and pens he can get his teeth on. And I think he ate a bar of Dove soap this morning.

My son can't come get him soon enough.

So why do I feel guilty saying that?

Tucker does have his halo moments. And if I take him outside to let him burn off some of that energy, he won't feel compelled to chew everything in sight. Okay, not everything.

He loves to chase a tennis ball but refuses to give it back to me. I don't have time for this "try to get the ball from me" game.

Then the other day I came up with a brilliant ploy: I used two tennis balls. When he came back with one (and refused to drop it), I showed him the other then tossed it. That went on until —glory, hallelujah!—he wore out and went up by the woods line and plopped down in the leaves.

But then we lost one of the tennis balls, so we're down to just one. And it's too cold and wet outside to stand there waiting for him to drop the ball so I can toss it again.

So he's stuck inside. With me. Who can't say no.

In her book *Conquering the Time Factor*, author Julie-Allyson Ieron examines twelve myths that steal time from us, one of which I'll address here: "If I turn you down, you'll think I don't value you, or worse, you'll be disappointed in me."

How many times do I say yes because I'm a people pleaser and don't like to disappoint others, even when it's an inconvenience (and even when it's a dog)? And more than an inconvenience—it prevents me from doing what I'm called to do.

Priorities come in play here. It's important to establish and maintain what's most important in your life and use this as a plumb line for what to say yes to and what to say no to.

My priories, in order of importance, are my relationship with God, my family, self-care, and my service to God.

I'm not sure where to put "self-care" because if I don't take care of myself, I can't take care of my family or serve God the best I can. It's like when the oxygen masks are deployed on a flight—you're to put yours on first then help someone else with theirs.

The same is true with nurturing my relationship with God by spending time with Him in prayer and His Word. I must feed my own spirit and grow my own faith first if I'm to help others with theirs and fulfill my calling.

It's okay to say no to things that don't clearly fit in any of these priorities. It's even okay to say no to family at times. Because sometimes I have deadlines. Because sometimes I just need me time. Because sometimes there's something more important to tend to. Remember the saying about not letting the urgent crowd out the important?

And, as Julie-Allyson points out, I don't have to explain why I say no. Like Jesus said, "Let your 'no' be 'no.'" That's it. No explanations necessary.

What about those times the lines are blurred, the times when what you're being asked to do doesn't clearly fit in your established priorities?

Pray for wisdom, and God will give it to you (James 1:5).

I'm not saying I have it all put together. I don't. I still struggle with saying no. I continue to wrestle with establishing and maintaining boundaries in my life.

But with God's help, my vision is becoming clearer and my focus sharper.

What about you? When do you need to just say no?

Father, grant me the wisdom to know when to say "no" and the discipline to decline. May the only one I strive to please be You. Amen.

MORE TEA: Read and reflect on Matthew 22:36–40.

Walling In or Walling Out?

You are a shield around me, O LORD. –Psalm 3:3 NIV

IN OLD TESTAMENT TIMES, walls surrounded cities, walls so thick houses were built into them. Today, instead of walls, we trust our security to the armed forces, police, and other groups created for our protection.

But walls still exist. The Great Wall of China, for instance, was constructed in the seventh century BC to protect the country from invasions and raids from nomadic groups to the north. Today the wall continues to defend the country against invaders on foot and serves as a border between China and the countries flanking it.

When it was built, however, China was not a communist nation, and the wall was not meant to keep citizens in, like the Berlin Wall.

Which brings me back to Frost's poem, "Mending Wall," and the line, "Before I built a wall I'd ask to know/What I was walling in or walling out."

We all build walls around us, don't we? Invisible walls to wall out the unwanted and to wall in that which we want to protect.

First, let's look at what we wall out.

I, for one, wall out toxic people—people whose behavior has a noxious effect on me, on my emotions, on my thinking, and consequently on my behavior. They spew their poison, and, like yeast, it permeates every aspect of my life if I let it.

I can't change these individuals, even if I tried. But I can pray for them. I can't love them on my own, but I can ask God to love them through me.

But that doesn't mean I have to spend time with them. After all, I'm only human. That's why I have to wall them out. So their poison doesn't affect me and those I love.

What other influences must I wall out? The godless and corrupt. Negative thinking. Negative speech. Anything that tears down and doesn't build up. That which discourages me, robs me of hope, siphons love, and undermines my faith. That which would distract and derail me from God's purpose for me.

What are we walling in?

That which we want to protect—our minds, our hearts, our spirits.

There's so much out there bent only to destroy. Remember what Jesus, the Good Shepherd who encloses His fold in a sheep pen, said? "The thief comes only to steal and kill and destroy; I have come that they may have life, and have it to the full" (John 10:10).

Walling in doesn't mean you have a closed mind but that you're protecting it from corrupting influences (Philippians 4:8–9, Romans 12:2). It doesn't mean that you become afraid to love, thinking that will protect your heart, but that you ask God to love others through you. Not your love, then, but His. Walling in your spirit doesn't mean you have a blind faith, but with single-minded devotion and commitment to God and His Word, you're protecting the garden of your faith so it can grow to full maturity and produce an abundant harvest.

Take a close look at your life.

What are you walling in and walling out?

Lord God, be the wall around me. Whatever You allow in, I know You have a purpose for it. Help me to live my life in Your sheep pen and trust my Shepherd. Amen.

MORE TEA:

Read and reflect on Matthew 13:31–33 and John 10:1–10.

Fruit of the Spirit

But the fruit of the Spirit is love, joy, peace, patience, kindness, goodness, faithfulness, gentleness, self-control.

–Galatians 5:22–23 ESV

Control Freak

But when the Holy Spirit controls our lives, he will produce this kind of fruit in us: love, joy, peace, patience, kindness, goodness, faithfulness, gentleness, and self-control. –Galatians 5:22–23 NLT

GROWING UP AS THE youngest in a poor family wasn't all that great.

I rarely got new clothes. Hand-me-downs from my older sister had to do, whether I liked them or not—and just about everything needed hemmed or taken in.

Then there was the keep-her-close-to-home syndrome my parents seemed to suffer from. Neither my brother nor my sister were rebellious in the sixties way, but, for some reason, my parents kept me close to home—and that included not wanting me to get a part-time job. A little pocket money would have improved my practically nonexistent social life, but my parents told me my job was "to be a good student" and "help your mother around the house."

I obeyed on both counts. I made the honor roll every grading period and cleaned the house every week during the summer months. One time, wanting something different, I rearranged my bedroom furniture, now that I had the room all to myself, then spent the evening at a friend's house. When I returned, the room was back the way it had been.

Then there was the financial situation. I'd been selected to be a band majorette for my junior year, and that meant money for boots, tassels, a new baton, band jacket, and a brand new uniform—and occasionally a soft drink after practice. My parents were still struggling from my father's layoff years earlier. Knowing it was hard for them to come up with the extra cash, I got a part-time job at the school library for the summer months. It was one of those underprivileged student jobs through the local government.

My first day was heaven. I loved the work—I mean, here I was, an avid reader, working in a *library*. And I loved feeling useful, doing something to contribute to the family finances.

But when I got home, my mother told me that I wouldn't be going to work the next day—or any day.

"There was a mistake," she said.

Once again, I obeyed, but when I landed my first teaching job years later, I seized the reins of my life. And have struggled with relinquishing them ever since—even to God. Even though I know His way is best and He's not a control freak like my mother was.

The kind of control my mother exerted led to frustration, disappointment, heartache, and rebellion.

But the kind of control that God, through His Holy Spirit, exerts leads to only good things—such as joy, peace, satisfaction, and fulfillment.

Isn't that what we all hunger for?

Dear God, when I fight You for my way, remind me that Your way leads to all I'm searching for, all I desire. Break the control freak in me. Amen.

MORE TEA: Read and reflect on John 15:1–8; 14:16–17, 26; 16:13.

That's What Parents Do

The fruit of the Spirit is love . . . –Galatians 5:23 RSV
We love, because He first loved us. –1 John 4:19 RSV

AT FIRST I THOUGHT I had a flat tire. I was on my way to Johnstown to take my college-age son to the doctor's. He'd called earlier, asking me what my schedule was for the day.

"I have a list of things to do," I said. "Why?"

"Never mind," he mumbled.

Turned out he needed a ride to the doctor's office because he couldn't shake a weeks-long bout with congestion and persistent coughing, and his car was in the repair shop—that is, *Dad's* repair shop, with possibly a blown motor. My husband had driven to Johnstown two days earlier to bring it home and, hopefully, fix it or get it fixed. At our expense, of course. Most college kids don't have the money it takes to fix cars. At least, ours didn't. He barely had enough to keep it running.

So I put aside my do-list, gathered the makings of homemade chicken soup, stuffed my checkbook in my purse, and headed for Johnstown. That's what parents do.

It was on the other side of Northern Cambria that I heard the *whoomp-whoomp-whoomp*. I pulled over, put on the four-ways, and got out. None of the tires, though, were flat. But as I walked in front of my eleven-year-old Explorer, which boasts nearly 164,000 miles, I heard what sounded like little stones hitting the inside of the hood. I checked the gauges—all were showing normal readings. The sound soon ceased, and, after checking the gauges again and listening to the engine, which sounded like it always does, I was on my way.

That evening, with half a tank of gas less than I had before my unexpected trip and $57 more on my credit card (for medicine—that's what parents do), I arrived home. My husband popped the hood, examined the engine, then came and got me.

"Look," he said, pointing to the belt that runs the engine and just about everything else.

It was split in half—but lengthwise, so that although half the belt was twisted up and useless, the other half still held, running the engine and getting me home safely.

"You ran on prayer," he said, scratching his head. "I don't know how that held."

Or how the broken half didn't twist around the motor, stopping everything, I thought. Then I grinned.

"My Father," I said, the warm fuzzy reaching from my heart to my lips, "takes good care of me."

You see, that's what parents do.

Dear God, thank You for Your awesome love for and care of me. It's exceedingly abundantly above all I can ask or imagine. Amen.

MORE TEA: Read and reflect on 1 John 4:7–21.

For more on God's love, read Romans 8: 31–39; Ephesians 3:17–20; Psalm 139; Psalm 103:11; Isaiah 43:4 … gee, the entire Bible is filled with His love for us!

The Joy Stealers

The fruit of the Spirit is ... joy. –Galatians 5:22 NIV

I know how to be abased, and I know how to abound; in any and all circumstances I have learned the secret of facing plenty and hunger, abundance and want. –Philippians 4:12 RSV

MY GRANDSON AND I had an interesting conversation in church one Sunday. The pastor was preaching on the Ten Commandments, and Brent, as usual, was on the fidgety side. So I gave him a notebook and pencil to help burn up some of that nervous energy. He spent the next several minutes copying the Ten C's in the notebook then showed it to me.

When I got to the last one, I noticed that "covet" looked like "cover." *I wonder if he knows what "covet" means?* I thought. At eight, probably not. So I asked him. (Writing in the notebook, of course. It wouldn't do to talk in church, and with my hearing loss, even with my hearing aid, I can't hear whispers.)

He shook his head.

"It means to want something that you don't have," I wrote. "To want something that belongs to someone else.

"It's a sin because it makes you feel jealous and envious of others—and ungrateful for what God has given you. It also leads to stealing, and it robs us of *joy*."

I underlined joy twice.

I don't know whether Brent understood what I was trying to teach him, but it sure gave me plenty to think about.

You see, the past couple of months had been lean as far as my freelance writing and editing go. It seemed as though everything had dried up. The outgo exceeded the income. And we needed both incomes—from my husband's job and my freelance work. And focusing on the debt was sucking the joy out of life.

So we decided to streamline and simplify. I canceled the DirecTV and the newspaper subscription, and dropped my Curves membership. Walking is cheaper and will give me the same results. I substituted skim milk for the expensive protein shakes I'd been drinking and warm skim milk at bedtime in place of ice cream.

I borrowed a relative's unused bread machine and began baking bread from scratch.

My husband was okay with this. "It's what you get used to," he told me with an I-really-don't-want-to-do-this-but-I-will-if-you-say-we-have-to look on his face.

I was okay with it, too. After all, I've spent most of my life on the "have not" side of things. It's taught me resourcefulness. And I love a challenge.

One day I pulled out my verse for the day—Philippians 4:12.

I'd always read that verse from the have-not perspective, but this time it hit me: I know how to be abased. I know how to face want and hunger. What I *don't* know is how to abound. How to handle plenty and abundance.

I've had the chance, and I was unwise. I took the plenty for granted, felt a false security in it, and wanted more—so I could keep up with others whom I secretly envied.

But the abundance didn't bring me the joy I thought it would. I worried that I'd lose it, that someone would steal it, or it would be burned in a fire or otherwise destroyed.

It may be that not having enough steals joy. But the more dangerous joy stealers are covetousness and not knowing how to handle the blessings we've been given.

Deep, lasting joy comes from knowing that God will supply all my needs according to His glorious, abundant, limitless riches (Philippians 4:19).

And that's a promise I can bank on!

Give me neither poverty nor riches, O Lord. Give me just enough to satisfy my needs. For if I grow rich, I may become content without You. And if I am too poor, I may steal, and thus insult Your holy name. Amen. (Proverbs 30:8–9)

MORE TEA: Read and reflect on James 4:1–8.

For more on joy and joy stealers, read Hebrews 13:5; Matthew 6; Philippians 4:4–7; Romans 12:12. And, when you're feeling down, sing a verse or two of "Count Your Blessings."

Games People Play

The fruit of the Spirit is . . . peace. Galatians 5:22 NIV

Do everything possible on your part to live in peace with everybody. –Romans 12:18 TEV

Make every effort to live in peace with all men. –Hebrews 12:14 NIV

KAREN AND PAULETTE WERE fighting again. Our third grade class was split in two.

"Whose side are you on?" one classmate would ask the other.

Never mind that the two best friends would soon make up and put the spat behind them, leaving the rest of us in social turmoil, everyone mad at everyone who wasn't on her side.

Everyone, that is, except Thomas.

"I'm on my own side," he answered confidently when I asked him.

Good for Thomas for not choosing sides and staying out of it. He probably had—and kept—the most friends.

Why did I have to choose a side, anyway? Because it was the thing to do? Because I felt pressured by my peers? Because if I didn't choose a side, I'd be left out? At least if I chose a side, I'd have *some* friends.

At that age, I thought the silliness of taking sides was a kid-thing, that we'd outgrow it and, as adults, be able to get along with one another.

Ha! It doesn't get any better, does it? From office squabbles to church splits to road rage to family feuds, discord abounds in the world around us. Will it ever end?

A more important question, though, is, where does it start? (Once you can answer where it starts, you have the answer to how it can end.)

It starts, not with conflict between two people, but in the heart. When the twins of selfishness and pride reign, one-upmanship defines all your relationships. You have to tell the better story, own the nicer home, drive the more expensive car, have the last word, inflict the final blow.

It never ends, though, does it? It just goes on and on and on, until one person says, "I've had enough."

It takes two to tangle. All it takes for peace is for one person to refuse to take part in these dangerous games people play.

Look at the story of King Saul and David, the shepherd boy anointed to be the next king. With all his kingly resources, Saul relentlessly pursued David to kill him, but David, even when he had an opportunity to gain the upper hand, refused to retaliate. It wasn't David who suffered from a troubled spirit (1 Samuel 16:14).

How can we obtain the inner peace that spills over into outer peace?

First, make peace with God, the giver of peace (Romans 5:1), through His Son, Jesus Christ. Remember the peace that He gives is deep and lasting, unaffected by worldly troubles (John 14:27).

Second, learn to trust God with every aspect of your life, banishing anxiety by telling God about your needs (Philippians 4:6–7, 19; Matthew 6:8, 25–33), knowing that His way is always the best way (Isaiah 55:8–9).

Third, train your mind so that your thoughts are on God, for He will "keep him in perfect peace whose mind is stayed on" Him (Isaiah 26:3).

Fourth, make a conscious effort to "let the peace of Christ rule in your hearts" (Colossians 3:15) by refusing to play the one-upmanship game, to retaliate when someone hurts you (Matthew 5:38–48). Don't allow bitterness to take root in your heart and mind, where it will grow and poison you and your relationships with others (Hebrews 12:14). "Get rid of all bitterness, rage and anger, brawling and slander, and every kind of malice" (Ephesians 4:31). Don't play the payback game (Romans 12:14–21).

Instead, "be kind and compassionate to one another, forgiving each other, just as God, in Christ, has forgiven you" (Ephesians 4:32), and overcoming bad with good.

Peace is a choice.

What's yours?

Dear God, in a time when world peace is humanly impossible, remind me that true peace begins with me—and You. Amen.

MORE TEA: Read and reflect on 1 Samuel 24; Colossians 3:12–15.

Hangeth Thou in There

The fruit of the Spirit is . . . patience. –Galatians 5:22 NIV

Do not throw away this confident trust in the Lord, no matter what happens. ... Patient endurance is what you need now, so you will continue to do God's will. Then you will receive all that he has promised. –Hebrews 10:35-36 NLT

"Any time a man takes a stand, there will come a time when he'll be tested to see how firmly his feet are planted." –Author unknown

IT ALL BEGAN WITH an email—one of those forwards I usually delete without opening. All my bad luck I can blame on deleting them, because most come with a curse or a guilt trip if I don't forward it to seven or ten or a hundred friends within seven minutes.

But this one I opened and scanned the contents. Then my eyes stopped. "God, deliver the person reading this right now from debt and debt burdens."

With a son in college and the escalating cost of living, it was getting harder and harder to keep our heads above water.

The following Sunday (Okay, I forwarded it to seven people, including the person who sent it to me—may the gods of cyberspace be appeased), I noticed in the church bulletin an announcement about a workshop for managing finances. "Get control of your finances. Get out of debt." I read.

"We're going," I told my husband.

After the workshop, we resolved to commit ourselves to getting our finances under control. And we started praying together every morning at 5:30 a.m. before Dean left for work.

At first things seemed to be going smoothly. Two unexpected checks came in that month to help the income meet the outgo. We came up with numerous, creative ways to tighten our belts, streamline and simplify.

Then our son's car—the one Dean worked on all summer and into which we'd poured hundreds of dollars—broke down. It was like a giant hand was pushing us back under water. For two weeks, Dean tinkered with it, trying to figure out what the problem was. Then he turned it over to an engine repair shop that still couldn't find the problem after two weeks.

We asked ourselves, "What's *this* going to cost?"

My freelance income had all but dried up.

The more I pray, the more I heard God telling me, over and over and over: *Be still. Wait. Be patient.*

Waiting is not one of my strong points, and patience is not a virtue I possess in abundance.

But everywhere I turned there it was: on the screen at church as we sang worship songs, on a bowl on a friend's coffee table, in my devotional readings—*Be still. Wait. Be patient.*

My journal pages filled up with Scripture that jumped out at me and insights that pierced my mind like a well-aimed arrow. One morning I wrote: "I want this time to be over quickly, learn the lesson, and move on to better things, out of the hole of debt. But God is doing a greater work in us.

"Our marriage relationship is becoming stronger. We've become closer as we discuss things and as we pray together every morning. We try to help each other out of the funk we get in when we focus on the mountain and not on the God who's bigger than the mountain. We're seeing more of what we have and less of what we don't have, what we truly need and what we could do without. And God is strengthening the 'do-without' so we don't miss what we've eliminated. He's showing us where we're weak and helping us to overcome those weaknesses.

"We're on the road to a better, stronger, more satisfying marriage; a simple, more satisfying lifestyle and a closer walk with God as we learn to depend on Him and trust Him more and more. This process takes time. I should not rush it. God knows what He's doing."

My part is to be patient.

Dear God, help me to hang in there. Remind me that what You have in store for us will be worth the wait. Amen.

MORE TEA: Read and reflect on James 1:2–4; 5:7–11.

Kindness Is ...

The fruit of the Spirit is ... kindness. –Galatians 5:22 NIV
Be kind to one another. –Ephesians 4:32 NIV

IN A SCENE IN the movie *The Notebook*, Allie, who is in the later stages of Alzheimer's disease, and Noah, whom she no longer remembers as her husband, are chatting in the extended care facility in which they now reside.

Noah recites a quote from a poem they once shared.

"That's beautiful," Allie says. "Did you write it?"

Noah smiles softly and answers, "No. Walt Whitman did."

Allie looks puzzled for a few seconds then says thoughtfully, "Walt Whitman. I think I knew him."

Noah smiles. "I think you did."

Now, if that were me, I probably would have launched into a mini-literature lesson. The teacher in me—or the parent—or the perfectionist—just can't squelch the urge to correct mistakes, to set the record straight.

But Noah doesn't correct Allie. Setting the record straight isn't important. Saving her from embarrassment and pain is. Throughout the movie, when Allie asks questions, Noah purposely gives evasive answers.

"On days like these, when her memory is gone, I am vague in my answers because I've hurt my wife unintentionally with careless slips of my tongue," he explains, "and I'm determined not to let it happen again."

I've done that—hurt other people unintentionally with words and deeds that I thought were helpful. It's not kind, for example, to correct all the typos and errors I see in the church bulletin. Even if no one else sees me scribbling away.

It's not kind to interrupt my husband's story because he got a couple of details wrong.

It's not kind to put my children down in front of others, remind them of past mistakes, make fun of their faults, or make them the butt of a joke.

Kindness is being sensitive to someone's feelings. It's helping another person to save face, couching the truth in cushions of love.

Kindness is finding something nice to say about your wife's appearance when the dress she's wearing *does* make her look fat.

Kindness is praising your husband's attempts at cooking supper and ignoring the overdone meat, the grease splattered three feet in every direction from the stove, and the kitchen that now looks like a disaster area.

Kindness is telling your daughter the floor needed mopped anyway when she puts dishwashing liquid in the dishwasher instead of dishwasher detergent.

Kindness is not calling your son an idiot after he fills up his gas tank with diesel fuel instead of gasoline.

Kindness is baking cookies for that neighbor who's meaner than a junkyard dog (Romans 15:7).

Kindness is saying something nice about someone who's not saying nice things about you (Proverbs 19:11).

Kindness is not judging the snippy receptionist in the doctor's office (Romans 14:13).

Kindness is encouraging that young mother struggling with busy toddlers in the grocery store (1 Thessalonians 5:11).

Kindness is praying for your son's girlfriend even though you think she's not good enough for him.

You can argue that Noah's kindness was born of love. True.

But as I thought about kindness, I realized that kindness and love are intertwined. One cannot be divorced from the other.

Perhaps that's why the word "fruit" in "the fruit of the Spirit" is singular.

Dear God, show me ways to be kind to others today. Amen.

MORE TEA: Read and reflect on the Book of Ruth.

Goody Two-Shoes—NOT!

The fruit of the Spirit is goodness. –Galatians 5:22 NIV

IT WASN'T MY MISTAKE, but I'm going to be the one to pay for it.

When my credit union changed hands last year, the new company changed the date on which it automatically deducted a three-hundred-dollar loan payment so that the payment would come out two days earlier.

The problem was they never told me. Never sent me a notice, never called me. Nothing.

So when I received a notice that they were docking my checking account fifty dollars for two bounced checks, I called.

"I mailed a check two days before the loan payment was due," I told them. "It was enough to cover the payment."

That's when they told me about changing the date. Long story short, they added the fifty dollars back in my account.

I thought that was the end of the matter until I got a bill from the optometrist for fifteen dollars—the insufficient funds fee from one of the checks my credit union bounced because they took out the loan payment two days early.

I called the optometrist's office and explained what happened.

"I'm not paying this," I said firmly. "This wasn't my fault."

You know the spiel. The bank charged them the fee, and they were passing it on to me.

I argued with the office manager.

"Somebody has to pay it," she insisted. "And we aren't."

"I shouldn't have to pay for someone else's mistake," I muttered to myself after I hung up.

Then I pictured the Son of God hanging on a cross. He paid for all of our mistakes. All of our rebellion. All of our wrongs. And He never did a thing wrong.

I called the office manager back and apologized.

"I get yelled at everyday," she told me, her voice softening. "It's not often someone calls back and apologizes."

I thought about calling the credit union or the bank involved and arguing my case with them, but decided it would be easier to pay the $15 than to run headfirst into the concrete wall of corporate policy. My blood pressure is high enough.

"To be good," reads my Bible dictionary, "is to do what is right. It is to show, by our works, praiseworthy character and moral excellence."

I'm no goody two-shoes. I fail every day. I get tired of doing the right thing time and time again, only to get slammed, blindsided, taken advantage of, and treated like I'm a nobody.

But that's why God gave me His Holy Spirit—to help me to do that which I know is right, especially when it's hard to do.

And sometimes the right thing is to say, "the buck stops here."

Dear God, forgive me for becoming weary in well-doing. Give me the wisdom to know the right thing to do and the strength and courage to do it. Amen.

MORE TEA:

Read and reflect on the following Scripture verses:

He has showed you, O man, what is good. And what does the LORD require of you? To act justly and to love mercy and to walk humbly with your God. –Micah 6:8 NIV

For we are God's workmanship, created in Christ Jesus to do good works, which God has prepared in advance for us to do. Ephesians 2:10 NIV

And let us not become weary in doing good, for at the proper time we will reap a harvest if we do not give up. Therefore, as we have opportunity, let us do good to all people, especially to those who belong to the family of believers. –Galatians 6:9-10 NIV

Of Kicks and Crowns

The fruit of the Spirit is ... faithfulness. – Galatians 5:22 NIV

Well done, good and faithful servant; you have been faithful over a little, I will set you over much; enter into the joy of your master. – Matthew 25:21 RSV

Work hard and cheerfully at whatever you do, as though you were working for the Lord rather than for people. ... the Master you are serving is Christ. –Colossians 3:23, 24 NLT

"I KNEW I SHOULDN'T have sent that manuscript evaluation before the guy paid me," I grumbled to my husband one night at the supper table. "Now I'll never get paid. What do I get for being nice? A kick in the pants."

"No," he said with a knowing smile. "Another jewel in your crown."

"And what about that book order I sent on good faith that the lady really did just put the check in the mail, like she claimed?" I continued, ignoring his comment. "Twenty-two bucks may not sound like a lot, but we could really use that money now."

He grinned. "Another jewel in your crown."

I wasn't in the mood to hear about jewels in my someday crown. We needed money in our checking account. My freelance work wasn't just slow—it had come to a screeching halt.

I thought of all the books and bookmarks I'd given away, the hours I'd spent—way more than I was paid for—painstakingly editing mediocre manuscripts because I felt each author deserved my best work. I thought of all the work I'd done *gratis*—articles written, workshops taught, manuscripts edited. I thought of all the recent opportunities for writing, speaking, and editing that had fallen through. I thought of the paying job doing something I loved that I gave up because I believed God called me to write full time. And now doors were slamming shut in my face.

Weren't you supposed to be rewarded for doing the right thing and being faithful?

"You know the verse about 'casting your bread on the waters and after many days, you'll find it again'?"

Sensing I was on a roll and nothing he could say would derail me, Dean didn't even nod.

"Well," I continued, "my bread must have gotten water-logged and sunk, or gobbled up by fish and fowl."

Faithfulness isn't easy. Especially when you've done all the Good Book says to do, and you don't see the fruit of your labors.

When you've trained up your children in the way they should go (Proverbs 22:6), and they choose not to follow it. When you've faithfully brought your tithe into the storehouse (Malachi 3:10), but the windows of heaven remain shut tight. When you're kind, thoughtful, and pleasant to people, treating them the way you want to be treated (Matthew 7:12), and they're snippy, rude, and thoughtless in return.

Sometimes I get tired of doing the right thing. Of being the nice guy. Nice guys get taken advantage of. They get ignored, overlooked. They're overworked and underpaid. And, like me, they sometimes become battle-weary and weak, vulnerable to doubt and despair.

We can give in or choose to fight the good fight of faith (1 Timothy 6:12), remembering that "He who called us is faithful" (1 Thessalonians 5:24) and will keep His Word (Isaiah 55:11). Even when we're faithless, God remains faithful because He cannot be false to Himself (2 Timothy 2:13).

These days I find myself repeating the words of Jim Cymbala: "Though in my heart I've questioned, even failed to believe, He's been faithful, faithful to me."

How can I be any less?

Dear God, I've poured my heart and soul into what You've called me to do, but, for all my labor, I see little, if any, fruit. I feel like such a failure. Help me to persist and persevere in the face of disappointment and discouragement and to leave the fruit up to You. Remind me that You have not called me to be successful, but to be faithful. Amen.

MORE TEA: Read and reflect on Matthew 25:14–46.

A Soft Answer

The fruit of the Spirit ... is gentleness. –Galatians 5:22, 23 NIV

A gentle answer turns away wrath, but a harsh word stirs up anger. –Proverbs 15:1 NIV

Let your gentleness be evident to all. –Philippians 4:5 NIV

"I HATE YOU!" SCREAMED my friend's little boy as she held him, squirming and kicking, in her lap and struggled to put sneakers on his busy feet. It was time to go, and the toddler didn't want the visit to end.

"Well," she answered gently, tying his shoelaces and planting a soft kiss on his cheek, "I love you."

I was amazed. If that were me, I would have turned him over my knee and spanked his little wriggling behind but good.

As a grandmother, I'm much gentler than I was as a mother, and in everyday life, I find I'm holding my tongue better than I used to—except when I'm behind the wheel of my vehicle or at one of my son's baseball games.

Every driver who doesn't use turn signals, passes in a no passing zone, tailgates me, slows me down by driving below the speed limit, or neglects to turn on the headlights when it's hard to see because of rain, snow, fog, or dusk, is, in my opinion, an idiot. While I don't succumb to road rage, my mouth goes a mile a minute and the words are none too gentle. Which is why I don't have one of those "Honk if you love Jesus" bumper stickers on my vehicle.

And at baseball games, it's hard to respond in a gentle manner when the umpire makes an obviously bad call that goes against the team I'm rooting for, especially in a close game where one call can change the momentum of the whole game. Before the last series, I promised God I'd behave and keep my mouth shut. But when the home plate umpire called one of our runners out at second after the base umpire had called him safe—and from my vantage point in the stands behind the plate, he *was* safe—I yelled that he was making it hard for me to keep my promise.

At that point my husband turned to me. I couldn't tell if he was embarrassed or amused.

"Behave yourself," he said, nodding to the seat in front of us, where our grandson Brent, who'had just started Little League, was booing. "You're not setting a good example."

So I kept my mouth shut and only groaned when the umpire called a homerun a foul ball. I gave him the benefit of the doubt and agreed with my husband that the foul pole needed to be higher.

"I hope this guy doesn't umpire any games for the playoffs," I couldn't resist adding.

I need to stop and consider what the other parents think when someone who claims to be a Christian yells at the umpire like I do. Bad calls are part of baseball, from Little League to the professional leagues. While it's okay to disagree, it's not okay to be disagreeable and unkind.

Being gentle means to treat others with kindness, consideration, and respect because, no matter who they are, they have value in God's eyes. Jesus set the example when He embraced the children the disciples tried to shoo away and when He had dinner with despised tax collectors who to the Jews were little more than scumbags, but to Him were hungry souls needing love, mercy, and grace.

Can I do any less?

Dear God, grow Your gentleness in me. Amen.

MORE TEA: Read and reflect on Ephesians 4:1–3.

Spout and Pout

The fruit of the Spirit is ... self-control. –Galatians 5:22–23 NIV

AT THE BEGINNING OF every year, I write out my goals for the coming year. In January, I noticed that "lose weight," "manage time better" and "get out of debt" were three recurring ones, going back years and years and years—and ones on which I'd made little, if any progress.

"Hmmm," I thought in a moment of brilliant self-revelation. "Looks like I have a little problem with self-control."

I've lost and gained the same fifteen pounds several times now.

Time management is almost as difficult. One of my weekly goals was "be more realistic in setting goals."

As far as the finances, well, we all know how impossible it seems to get out of the hole once you're in.

But I'd been making progress—slow, but inching ahead—until I overdrew the checking account. I'd scheduled a credit card payment to be made on the due date, figuring one of my writing checks would cover it. Normally it would have, but the check was a week late. And I'd forgotten about the payment.

When I went online to balance the account and noticed the $25 overdraft charge, I was sick—especially when I noticed that it had been deducted within the past hour.

I was mad. Mad at myself. But madder at God.

"I've been trying so hard, Lord," I complained. "And I've been doing so well. How could You do this to me?"

And I'd had such a good attitude earlier that same week when an order for one hundred of my books fell through. "Oh, well," I said at the time. "That's the way the cookie crumbles."

Then came the overdraft—and this cookie crumbled.

"It isn't my fault the check was late," I whined to God. "And, in regard to that canceled book order, I didn't count my chickens before they were hatched. The guy said in the spring he wanted the books. It was only last week that I noticed the money would have nicely taken care of the fall taxes, the heating oil, and the car insurance. How could You do this to me?"

I spouted. I pouted. I spouted some more. I still maintained my peace about the book order, but I stewed and spewed about the overdraft.

It took several days of complaining to the Almighty that it wasn't my fault, I had no control over when the check came in, but He did. Yada, yada, yada.

Somewhere during one of my non-spewing moments, it occurred to me that if I'd put some money aside as a cushion, to cover the payment should a check come late, instead of living from paycheck to paycheck, I'd have avoided the overdraft.

Okay, so I knew that all long. I just wouldn't admit it.

So now I'm trying to squirrel away a little bit every payday in a cushion fund.

Live and learn. Even when you're a golden-ager.

The Fruit of the Spirit—love, joy, peace, patience, gentleness, goodness, meekness, faith, and self control. I think I've struggled most with that last one.

I still do.

Dear God, I tend to forget that everything You allow in my life has a purpose. Thank You for reminding me. Amen.

MORE TEA:

Read and reflect on Galatians 5:22–23 and Psalm 40.

Parables

And He taught them many things in parables.

–Mark 4:2 AMP

This Little Light of Mine

"Let your light shine." – Jesus, as quoted in Matthew 5:16 NIV

I REMEMBER THE MOMENT clearly. A spanking new student teacher, I stood in front of a classroom for the first time. Perhaps I was a bit nervous. I don't remember. What I do remember is, at that moment, a light went on inside me—and has never gone out.

I'd found my calling—the purpose for which I was created—and joy flooded my soul.

The road to that moment wasn't easy. Growing up in the shadow of a gifted and popular older sister, I struggled with self-confidence and wormed my way through an identity crisis before the term was even coined. It didn't help that I looked and sounded like Judy (I didn't think so, but everyone else did).

In school, teachers wondered why I didn't get the grades Judy did. And I wondered why my classmates didn't like me as much her classmates liked her. Mine mockingly called me "Miss Popularity." When we got older and the boys started coming around—not for me, of course—I found it to my advantage that our voices sounded alike over the phone.

It wasn't until college—and nearly a hundred miles from my hometown, where no one knew Judy existed—that I finally found myself. I didn't have to bask in anyone else's light. I was free to shine my own.

But old habits die hard. In the let's-mock-Michele years, I'd learned it was better to hide in a corner than risk attention if I let my light shine too brightly. People have a way of putting you in what they think is your place—and it isn't to outshine them. I found that if I was too good at what I did, people would get envious and not like me. And I wanted to be liked. Besides, I thought hiding in a corner, not letting my light shine, was being humble.

Is that why God created me? Or you? To hide in a corner? Has He not given each person at least a seed of talent that we are to develop and use for Him (Matthew 25:14–30)? And hasn't He given each of us a special place in His kingdom? A unique job to do? And hasn't He given us what we need to accomplish that job? (1 Corinthians 12:7; Ephesians 4:7-13)

"You are the light of the world," He said. Wait a minute—isn't Jesus the Light of the World? Yes, He is. But His physical presence is no longer on this earth. Instead, He shines through each of His followers, who are to take His light to a world where moral decay and selfish lifestyles create an ever-increasing darkness.

We are not to hide the light He has put in us under busyness (the jar/vessel in Luke 8:16 represents work) or beneath idleness (the bed). Nor are we to bury the special abilities He has planted in us.

So don't be afraid to let your light shine, Child of God. That's why He created you.

Dear God, let Your light shine in and through me. Amen.

MORE TEA: Read and reflect on Matthew 5:14–16.

A Piece of the Rock

"Anyone who listens to my teaching and obeys me is wise, like a person who builds a house on solid rock." – Jesus, as quoted in Matthew 7:24 NLT

WHEN MY HUSBAND WOKE up one Sunday morning with his left arm numb, our life together suddenly took a different perspective. Especially when the numbness settled in his fingers on both hands and in his right foot. Uncertainty crept into our schedules just as sure as the doctors' appointments and plethora of medical tests.

Possible causes swirled through my mind. I spent hours online, searching WebMD and other sites, seeking understanding, trying to prepare myself for the worst.

Would he be able to continue to drive truck? Should we start thinking about another line of work? But then, what can you do when you lose the use of your fingers? Just three months earlier I had quit my full-time job, with its regular, although meager, paycheck. My freelance work was bringing in enough to help pay the bills, but that depended on how much work I contracted and when I received payment. So far, we were able to pay the bills on time.

I wasn't worried about the finances, though. I believed that the One who called me into full-time writing was faithful, and I trusted that He would provide for all our needs (1Thessalonians 5:24, Philippians 4:19). I knew that if Dean couldn't work anymore, then God would send enough work my way that I'd be able to support us both.

I was more concerned about losing my life's companion. With the kids grown up and gone, we'd gotten closer. I loved the stage of life we were in. Then the dreams of growing old together were suddenly threatened. But I had no real fear, no doubt, no anxiety. I slept well.

I was feeling pretty proud of my spiritual maturity when God dropped a bombshell: "You thought it was a leap of faith when you quit your job and trusted Me to provide. But would you still trust Me if your husband's paycheck were gone?"

My faith hadn't really been put to the test when I quit my job. I still had Dean, he still had his job, and the paychecks were still coming in. As long as I had those, faith talk was easy. Take all that away, and would I be able to walk my talk?

What can we place our security in these days? Certainly not in jobs. In insurance policies? They don't prevent misfortune; they only promise to provide for our needs in the event something happens. A good credit rating? Identity theft can shoot that overnight. A healthy bank account, investments? A sudden, catastrophic accident or illness, or an extended stay in a skilled care facility can eat those up quickly. Real estate? A house? A fire can destroy in a few minutes what we've spent a lifetime building. (Examples: Louisiana sliding into the Gulf, beach erosion, fire destroying mansions in Malibu).

Where, then, can we find true, rock-solid security? The Bible tells us, over and over: In God and in God alone. "The LORD is my rock," (Psalms 18:2, 19:4, 92:15; Isaiah 26:4; Deuteronomy 32:4).

I have a piece of the Rock. Do you?

Thank you, Lord, that You are the Rock upon which I build my life. Thank You that I'm no longer building on sand. Amen.

MORE TEA: Read and reflect on Matthew 7:24–27.

Clean Out the Closet!

When someone becomes a Christian, he becomes a brand new person inside. He is not the same any more. A new life has begun! –2 Corinthians 5:17 TLB

I KNEW I WAS overdue to clean out my clothes closet when I tried on three outfits for church one Sunday morning and none of them would do.

My wardrobe included three pairs of polyester slacks that I'd worn nearly every week for ten years (I exaggerate not) and that were coming apart at the seams, missing buttons at the waist, and were way too baggy since I'd lost some weight. My sweaters were fuzzbally, nearly transparent in places, or had shrunk in the wash. Most of my skirts, blouses, and dresses were tired and lifeless and looked like I felt. And most everything was way outdated.

Over the years, I'd added a piece or two to my wardrobe here and there, but, instead of removing anything to make room in my four-foot-wide closet, I simply shoved the old stuff back where it was hard to reach. My dresser drawers weren't much better. I had to iron anything before I wore it.

Finally I decided it was time. No more hanging on to stuff in case I lost weight or in case I'd want to wear it someday. No more "fat" and "skinny" wardrobes.

My tastes were changing, too. Instead of prints (usually flowers), I wanted solids in shades that complimented my coloring and in styles that complimented my body shape.

So after a day-long shopping trip and another day-long closet-cleaning session, I had fifty empty hangers, two empty dresser drawers, a healthy donation for Goodwill, and an equally healthy donation for the garbage man—and a feeling of being set free.

Every time I wear one of my new outfits, I feel like a new woman, lighter and happier than I've felt in years. Amazing how hanging on to useless old things can bog us down.

We do the same spiritually, don't we? Those old sins are hard to let go because we have a hard time believing we are truly forgiven and so we refuse to forget. We won't forgive ourselves, so we carry around a load of guilt, thinking this is our penance.

Is that what God does? No!

When we asked for His forgiveness and accepted His Son, we were changed inside. Not patched up, like a garment that needs mending. We were born again (John 3:16), given new life—His life in us. We became not fixed-up versions of our old selves, but brand new persons!

We were washed completely clean (1 John 1:9). *All* our sin-stain was bleached out entirely by the Son, and our hearts are now as white as snow (Isaiah 1:18, Psalm 51:2,7). All the garbage of sin and guilt was flung as far from us as the east is from the west (Psalm 103:12), and God remembers it no more (Jeremiah 31:34).

So why do we? Perhaps because we feel unworthy? But God considered us worthy enough to send His Son to die in our place and open the way to Heaven.

So, Christian, clean out your closet and toss the fuzzbally attitudes, oversized guilt, outdated shame. Don your new clothes—clothes as clean, fresh, and new as a spring morning—clothes that will make you feel like a new person—because, Child of God, you really are.

Create in me a clean heart, O God, and put a new and right spirit within me. Restore to me the joy of my salvation. Amen. (Psalm 51:10,12)

MORE TEA: Read and reflect on Matthew 9:14–17.

Soil Toil

Today, if you hear his voice, do not harden your hearts. – Psalm 95:7–8 NIV

EVERY YEAR WHEN IT'S time to plant our garden, my husband works hard to prepare the soil for the seeds.

First he plows, turning the hardened earth over and under. Then he tills it, breaking up tough clumps of sod and removing the rocks that rise to the surface with the churning—and there are buckets full still, after forty years. Then he works lime and fertilizer in the loose soil with the tiller—and, of course, removes more rocks.

Only when the soil is loose and porous, and boosted with nutrients necessary for plant growth does he drop in the seeds.

Even then his soil toil is far from over. Throughout the growing season, he must keep working it, tilling it to keep it loose and soft, plucking those endless rocks, pulling weeds, and periodically adding more lime and fertilizer.

After every hard rain, the soil hardens again, more rocks appear, and he must hoe around the growing plants so the nutrients they need to grow could filter through to the roots. And, of course, pick rocks.

Even after the harvest the work isn't done. Plowing the whole thing under allows the decaying plants to add more nutrients to the soil over the winter.

Then, the following spring, he starts all over. The ground always needs work.

Just like our souls. We need a lot of work, too—over and over. The work is never done on this earth.

It all starts with a hardened heart that cannot accept the seed. To get our attention, God often turns our lives upside-down, breaking up tough clumps of stubbornness and rebellion. Then, to soften our hearts even more, He keeps things churned up until we are submissive and workable. Rocks of selfishness and willfulness, which crop up daily, must be removed. Storms of life also tend to bring them to the surface.

But the seed needs nutrition to grow, and too many idle years result in a depleted soul, fallow and barren. To remedy this, the lime of prayer and the fertilizer of fellowship with more mature Christians must be applied—by the bagful.

But we're not ready to produce a harvest yet, are we? Those weeds of worldliness must be carefully twisted out of our hearts, where their roots reach deep, leeching the nutrients and choking the tendrils of spiritual life.

Only after all this toil—plowing, tilling, hoeing, rock plucking, fertilizing, watering, weeding—can our soil-soul support growth and eventually produce a harvest.

But there is never, really, any one type of soil, is there? Perhaps that's why I've always had trouble answering the question, "What kind of soil are you?"

I am not one type of soil, you see. I am all of them.

Dear God, thank You that soil can be changed. Thank You for changing me—little by little, rock by rock, weed by weed. Amen.

MORE TEA: Read and reflect on Matthew 13:3–9, 18–23.

Tales of Tares

"Let both grow together until the harvest." – Jesus, as quoted in Matthew 13:30 NIV

OY, WHAT A WORLD we live in! Just booting up my computer for the day's work can be depressing. I check my email first. Thank heavens for spam filters, which separate the wheat from the chaff, so to speak. I have it set on the highest setting, but still some garbage sneaks through, especially all the offers for Viagra and such. Then there are the forwards with the dire warnings of bad luck if I don't pass them on. Phooey on them all. Once in a blue moon I'll read one. Today I did.

It was from my brother, and it was about jury duty. Seems that some shysters are calling folks, posing as court officials and telling them there's a warrant out for their arrest because they didn't report for jury duty. When the innocent party protests that they never even received a summons, the con on the other end tells them he'll check into it, just give him your Social Security number and date of birth. Sometimes they even ask for a credit card number. Give them the information they want, and the nightmare of identity theft follows. (Check the validity of scams online at snopes.com.)

Then there are the Yahoo headlines, equally depressing. While most of them are about the Middle East mess (and all political propaganda to manipulate the public's opinion of the current administration), once in awhile there's something about the USA. Today there was one about the hype in Boston back in 2007. City officials were livid—the article's word, not mine—over an advertising campaign for a late-night television program. Seems that the broadcasting company put up electronic signs on bridges and other obvious places—thirty-eight in all—of a blinking cartoon character giving passersby an obscene gesture. This led to shutting down highways, bridges, and a section of the Charles River, sending in the bomb squad and costing the city a half a million dollars.

"Commerce was disrupted, transportation routes were paralyzed, residents were stranded and relatives across the nation were in fear for their loved ones in the city of Boston," said the Boston DA.

The mayor called the ploy an outrageous marketing scheme fueled by corporate greed. Well, yeah, isn't greed what makes the world go 'round these days?

And, speaking of sickos, you better make sure you have a good antivirus program installed and don't ever, ever let the subscription run out. Oh, and don't forget the firewalls to prevent hackers from breaking into your computer files and stealing sensitive financial information.

Then there are the block lists to are supposed prevent corporate greed from giving you indigestion at dinnertime, the filth you have to wade through to find a decent program on television, the obscene and offensive t-shirts and bumper stickers. It's enough to make me want to head for the hills and become a mountain woman.

Jesus warned there'd be times like this. Evil, sad to say, is here to stay, and evildoers aren't going anywhere, either. Jesus called them tares—actually "darnel," a weed that looked just like the wheat when it first sprouted. Only as the plants matured did the identity of the good seed and the bad seed become evident.

When you look around, Christian, and it seems that the tares are rampant, don't despair. Instead, rejoice in your hope, be patient in tribulation, and be constant in prayer (Romans 12:12) because, you see, the harvest *is* coming.

Dear God, sometimes I feel helpless and overwhelmed by the evil in the world around me. Help me to be a sturdy strand of wheat in a field of tares. Amen.

MORE TEA: Read and reflect on Matthew 13:24–30, 36–43.

A Little Leaven, A Lotta Heaven

"The kingdom of God is within you." –Jesus, as quoted in Luke 17:21 NKJV

FRIDAY NIGHT AT OUR house is-pizza-and-a-movie night. It began when the youngest left for college, and my husband and I ate out at a local pizzeria. Eventually our date night morphed into dining on frozen pizza at home. After a while frozen pizza lost its appeal, and I rooted around in my recipe box and retrieved my old pizza dough recipe.

Years ago I learned the secret of making good pizza dough. It's in the kneading. First I dissolve the yeast in warm water. Warm, not hot, because hot will kill the yeast. Then I add the sugar, salt, and oil, mixing it well so the yeast, sugar, and salt dissolve. Then I add about half the flour, mixing it with a wooden spoon until it's just past the gooey stage. Then I knead in the rest of the flour by one-half cupfuls—and I don't pay attention to the recipe! I pay attention to the dough. I'm done adding flour when the dough is just past being sticky, soft like a baby's behind, and springs back when I lightly indent it with my finger. I rarely use all the flour the recipe calls for.

Now, you're asking, what does this have to do with the kingdom of heaven? Everything. You see, Jesus spent a lot of time teaching the people about the kingdom of heaven, or the kingdom of God, using analogies of things they understood so they would grasp what He was trying to tell them.

"The kingdom of heaven," He said once, "is like yeast that a woman took and mixed into a large amount of flour until it worked all through the dough" (Matthew 13:33 GW). The kingdom of heaven is like yeast. The older versions use the word "leaven." Leaven, according to my trusty Webster's, is "any influence spreading through something and working on it to bring a gradual change." In bread dough, the leaven causes it to raise and gives it a delectable flavor. Ever eat bread that failed to raise? It's useless, isn't it? Fit only for the trashcan.

In this world, the leaven is the kingdom of heaven, or the rule of God over all who accept and submit to Him (see John 3:3,5). In each believer, the leaven is the words of the Master, found in Scripture, that gradually spread through our minds and hearts, transforming us, transforming our lives, ever so gradually.

First, though, the leaven must be added carefully then worked through the dough of our lives. Just like bread dough, the secret is in the kneading. Ever knead dough? It takes time and patience—and just the right touch—not too heavy and not too light.

God is the one who kneads His Word through our lives. If you're dough being kneaded, though, it doesn't feel too good to be twisted and turned and folded and pushed and pulled. But the Master knows what He's doing. He's not following a recipe because we are individual lumps, each needing a different touch, a different amount of flour to be added, and a different amount of kneading time. The Master works us until we're pliable, soft, resilient—not too sticky or gooey and not too dry or tough. Then He sets us aside for a while for the leaven to do its work.

But we're still not ready. Like bread dough, we must be punched down, worked again, shaped, and left alone, covered with a soft cloth, so that the leaven can finish its work. It's a long process.

Child of God, are you being kneaded? Don't despair. Just remember—a little bit of leaven, worked just right into the dough of your soul, means a whole a lot of heaven.

Dear God, thank You for kneading me in the way I need to be kneaded. Amen.

MORE TEA: Read and reflect on Matthew 13:33; Luke 17:20–21.

The Money Pit

"The kingdom of heaven is like treasure hidden in a field." – Jesus, as quoted in Matthew 13:44 NIV

ONE SUMMER DAY IN 1795, young Daniel McGinnis found what appeared to be a depression in the ground. The teenager, who lived on a small island off the coast of Nova Scotia called Oak Island, knew the area was reputed to have been frequented by pirates. Oak Island was one of three hundred small isles in the Mahone Bay, perfect for hiding pilfered treasures. So Daniel returned the next day with two of his friends and started digging.

He never found anything. What he did do, though, was spark a treasure hunt that spanned two hundred years, cost millions of dollars, and claimed half a dozen lives, including a daredevil motorcyclist and his eighteen-year-old son in 1959.

Excavators, digging and drilling to nearly two hundred feet, discovered charcoal, putty, spruce platforms, oak chests, layers of wood and iron, coconut fibers, parchment, loose pieces of metal, a cement vault, a human hand, a mysterious inscription on a stone, a flood tunnel, booby traps—but no treasure.

What really lies at the bottom of what's called the Money Pit? Treasure buried by Captain Kidd, who used the area for R

& R and to repair his ships? The original works of Shakespeare or Sir Francis Bacon? The crown jewels of France, which vanished four years before McGinnis stumbled onto the site? The long-lost Holy Grail? Or is the Money Pit nothing more than an old ammo dump?

No one knows. But who can resist the lure of buried treasure? Note the popularity of films such as *National Treasure* and *Pirates of the Caribbean*. Why do such stories appeal to us? Perhaps because we all harbor a secret dream that we will find a treasure that will make us rich beyond our wildest dreams. What wouldn't we give for a chance at it?

That's why Jesus used this analogy in describing the kingdom of heaven.

"The kingdom of heaven," He said, "is like treasure hidden in a field." Since there were no banks in the first century, it wasn't uncommon to hide treasure in the ground. If the person who buried it died without disclosing the whereabouts of his cache, it was finders, keepers.

"When a man found it," Jesus continued, "he hid it again, and then went and sold all he had and bought that field."

That's how valuable the kingdom of heaven is. The late missionary Jim Elliot understood this.

"He is no fool who gives that which he cannot keep to gain that which he cannot lose," he once said. Elliott was one of five missionaries murdered by the Auca Indians in 1956.

Mother Teresa also understood this, as did Hudson Taylor. And William Tyndale. And many others like them who gave all they had in order to serve the King. They knew that what they relinquished was minuscule compared to what they received—the kingdom of heaven. They gave that which they could not keep to gain that which they could not lose.

Now, that doesn't mean we have to run off and become missionaries when we submit to the rule of King Jesus. But it does mean that our priorities change. Our perspective changes. What we once thought was so important no longer is. It means that, like Paul, we say, "Everything else is worthless when compared with the priceless gain of knowing Christ Jesus my Lord. I have discarded everything else, counting it all as garbage, so that I may have Christ" (Philippians 3:8 NLT).

What about you—where is *your* treasure?

Dear God, I still cling to things that moth and rust can destroy, and thieves can steal. Remind me daily of where my real treasure lies. Amen.

MORE TEA:

Read and reflect on Matthew 13:44; Philippians 3:7–8.

Panicked Parent

"In the same way, heaven will be happier over one lost sinner who returns to God than over ninety-nine others who are righteous and haven't strayed away!" –Jesus, as quoted in Luke 15:7 NLT

MY TWO-YEAR-OLD son was missing. He'd climbed the back of the sofa in the downstairs family room and slipped out of an unscreened ground floor window while I washed windows upstairs and his older brother and sister, who were supposed to keep an eye on him, watched cartoons.

We lived at the edge of a small rural village on what used to be the family farm. Where could he be on this warm, spring afternoon? Traipsing in the acres of woods and overgrown fields? Climbing the high wall, a steep, dangerous cliff left from open-pit mining years ago? Exploring the barn filled with suffocating hay bales or the wagon shed with all its enticing tools and machines? I imagined a small body floating on the pond fifty yards away and felt panic rise like bile in my throat.

The world can be a dangerous place for a curious toddler. Fear clutched my heart and squeezed hard. I called around the neighborhood while Todd and Jaime began searching. A neighbor boy hopped on his four-wheeler.

I can't remember how long we searched. I only remember praying, pleading with God to help us find him safe and sound. We did—between the back doors of his grandmother's house next door. She wasn't home, so no one heard his knocking or answered the phone when I called.

What relief and joy flooded me when they brought him through the door! I hugged him and kissed him and hugged him some more.

There's nothing worse than not knowing where your children are. My children knew the degree of punishment was proportional to the degree of panic.

Unlike us, though, God doesn't panic when His children wander off. He always knows exactly where they are and goes after them. Not with punishment in mind, but in love and concern. He knows it's a mean, dangerous world out there.

And He never forces them to return against their will. Instead, He calls to them gently, softly whispering their names so they hear it deep in their souls. He arranges circumstances to get their attention. Cecil Murphey, in his books *The Relentless God* and *The God Who Pursues*, describes his own wandering and how God sought him, found him, and brought him home. My own Uncle Nick woke up in a jail cell after a drinking bout and found the Shepherd waiting for him. He became a Baptist minister who eventually led several family members to a deeper, more meaningful relationship with God.

Sometimes God sends others to bring home His beloved children. My friend Melanie wrote a book called *The Apostles He Sends,* describing how God sent others to draw her back to her faith after more than three decades of running away.

He never stops caring. He never stops loving us. He never stops seeking us when we stray. So whether you or someone you love is the little lost lamb, be assured that God knows where His lost ones are—and He's working on bringing them home.

Thank You for never letting me out of Your sight, Father, and thank You for bringing me home. Amen.

MORE TEA: Read and reflect on Matthew 18:12–14; Luke 15:3–7.

Keeping Score

"Forgive us the wrongs we have done, as we forgive the wrongs that others have done to us." – Matthew 6:12 TEV

"LORD," PETER ONCE ASKED Jesus, "how often should I forgive someone who sins against me? Seven times?"

Peter was being generous. Seven times was going above and beyond the call of duty. According to Jewish teaching, a man was to forgive someone four times. After that, forgiveness wasn't required.

Jesus' answer rocked Peter. "No. Seventy times seven!"

That's a lotta offenses. If you want to take this literally, get a notebook and jot down when someone says or does something to hurt you. Make sure you number the offenses—because when you get to 491, you can justify your unforgiving heart.

Sound ludicrous? Think about it. Don't we all keep score? Just get into an argument with someone, and out pours a litany of times that person offended you (or you offended him). True forgiveness doesn't come easy.

I can think of two times in my professional life when I found forgiveness difficult: when I was cheated out of a job and when a father turned a parent-teacher conference into an attack on me.

The first offense took years for me to get past. But eventually I saw that harboring bitterness was destroying me. Although I haven't forgotten, I don't dwell on the injustice—that only serves to stir up anger and hurt. Besides, once God's plan and purpose were revealed, I saw that it was much better than what I'd wanted at the time.

The second offense still smarts. I was explaining my position to the parent, a professing Christian prominent and active in the church, but my words were skillfully twisted and used against me. I can still feel the anger and frustration, the feelings of helplessness and futility.

One time I bruised my arm, but it didn't turn black and blue right away. As the days went by, though, the bruise turned darker and uglier. The deeper the bruise, someone told me, the longer it takes to come out.

The same with bruises to our hearts (and, okay, our egos). Only time can ease the pain, mellow the sharpness, sweeten the bitterness.

But we have a choice: Dwell on the injustice and the hurt, or "think" and "thank"—think only good things about the one who offended us (Philippians 4:8) and then thank God for the person, for his positive qualities, for the good that God will work out of what we think of as bad (Romans 8:28).

For a long time afterward, I felt a twinge of pain and anger every time I saw this parent. But I refused to dwell on what happened. Instead I thought of the many ways God blessed this man and is using him in His kingdom, and then I thanked Him.

You know what, now I can't even remember who he was.

That's the best way to keep score.

Dear God, You have commanded us to forgive. It's not an option. Help me to forgive others as You have forgiven me. Replace the anger and pain in my heart with Your love. And if I can't love the person who hurt me, then I give You permission to love him through me. Amen.

MORE TEA: read and reflect on Matthew 18:21–35.

Lazarus at My Gate

"Seek ye first the kingdom of God and His righteousness." – Jesus, as quoted in Matthew 6:33 KJV

GLOBAL SEEMS TO BE the latest buzz word. You've got to think, speak, and act globally. No more the small-town mindset. Anyone who isn't sophisticated, well-informed, and technology-savvy just isn't with it these days.

This global philosophy has infiltrated the Christian ranks, too. We're to pray for the world, for the country, for worldwide missions, for people we don't know and probably never will. Now, this isn't bad. Someone needs to pray for world peace and give to missions.

There are those who can handle this information overload. I'm not one of them.

Quite frankly, it depresses me. I'm overwhelmed by prayer lists that grow longer and more disheartening by the day. I feel helpless when I read of a 101-year-old woman on her way to church who's mugged by an addict who targets elderly women to get his drug money; of children and animals that are tortured and killed; of government officials who are more interested in playing politics, posturing, and pointing fingers than running the country; of misused money that was sent in good faith to alleviate others' suffering. Do I really need to know all this? My global prayers seem weak, bumbling, pat, and ineffective.

I keep thinking of the question God asked Moses, "What is that in your hand?" (Exodus 4:2) and the need to focus on what I have in my hand and do it well. I'm sensing the need to reach out to people around me who are hurting—something I've neglected because I've been too focused on the global.

But God has been saying, "Look to the Lazarus at your gate." The older I get, the more people I know will be hospitalized, lose loved ones, experience crises. These are the Lazaruses at my gate. Yet I've insulated and isolated myself from my immediate world in pursuit of the global.

How many decades did Mother Teresa labor in the ghettos of India unnoticed? Now, this woman didn't think globally. Yet her words resonate in my soul: "God has not called me to be successful; He has called me to be faithful."

When we focus too much on the global, we can overlook the people around us—family, neighbors, those we meet at church, in the store, at ballgames, and on the street—because we may think that ministering to them is too small. But the globe is made up of folks like these, and if we each reached out and touched them, the ripples will be felt in all the world.

Dear God, open my eyes to the Lazarus at my gate today. Amen.

MORE TEA: Read and reflect on Luke 16:19–31.

Wait 'Til Your Father Gets Home

If you, O LORD, keep a record of sins, who could stand? But with you there is forgiveness. Psalm 130:3–4 NIV

"WAIT 'TIL YOUR FATHER gets home" was not a threat I was able to use on my children. Their father, you see, was—and still is—a softy. I was the bad guy who doled out punishment and discipline.

But there was one time I was sure this easygoing husband of mine would crack and lose his temper with an errant, strong-willed, rebellious child.

One evening when my daughter was in high school, I'd taken her to the mall to do some school shopping. She'd just about finished when my aching feet drove me to the car to wait while she picked up some makeup. I waited. And waited. And waited. The mall was closing down and still no daughter. Where was she?

I returned to the store to find out. Well, she'd picked up some makeup, all right—and tried to get out of the store without paying.

I was beyond furious. How could she do something like this? How could she do this *to me*? I mean, after all, I was a Sunday school teacher and Bible club teacher, choir director, Christian writer. Wasn't I supposed to have perfect Christian children? What would people say? What would they think of me? *I'll never forgive her for this!* I vowed silently as I drove home, shaking with rage.

"When we get home," I hissed, "you will tell your father what you've done."

I sent her in ahead of me so I could try to calm down and give her time to tell him without me there. But when I walked in, the scene that greeted me was not what I'd had in mind. There, curled up in her father's lap, was our remorseful child.

I was stunned. How could he open his arms to her after what she'd done? How could he forgive her just like that? At that moment I don't know who I was madder at—her or him.

That was more than twenty years ago. Since then, our daughter has grown up to be quite the woman—wife, mother, fulltime student with close to a 4.0 GPA, and now an awesome high school math teacher. She received her college's "Heart of Gold" award for her work with a support group for parents of autistic children.

It took me years before I recognized what I really saw that night when I walked in the house: a perfect picture of God's unconditional love for us.

Thank You, Abba Father, that we can curl up in Your lap any time we need forgiveness. Amen.

MORE TEA: Read and reflect on Luke 15:11–32.

Like a Good Neighbor

"The second most important commandment is this: 'Love your neighbor as you love yourself.' There is no commandment more important than these two." –Jesus, as quoted in Mark 12:31 GNT

WHO WOULD HAVE THOUGHT a little thing like a sprayer hose separating from the cold water pipe under the kitchen sink would cause such a mess? And, to boot, the phones, mysteriously, weren't working, so my daughter-in-law couldn't call for help.

She'd just seen her oldest off to school and had two sleeping children upstairs, one of which was a four-month-old, when it happened. Her husband was two hours away on a job.

Of course she was upset when she came to use my phone. (We lived next door.) I remembered the panic, fear, and helplessness I felt when something went kerflooey and my husband was too far away to do anything about it. Laundry, cleaning, cooking, and patching up boo-boos were my territory, not wiring, plumbing, and heating.

I followed her to the house. Water spouted from the separated joint under the kitchen sink, drenching the cleaning supplies stored there, and cascading across the carpeted floor. The basement was no better. Dodging indoor raindrops, I tiptoed through the water streaming across the cement floor and located the electric box above the churning pump. Would I get electrocuted if I reached up and flipped the switch while standing in a pool of running water? I pulled the lever down. The pump shut off. I was still alive.

Now what? There was a mess to clean up, that's what. Rather than bustling around, getting in the way, though, I decided it would be better to give Rachael a little space—we women need time to work things through emotionally. I figured when my husband came home from work later in the day, we'd tackle the flood cleanup.

But when I returned an hour later with brownies (chocolate always helps in crisis situations), towels were spread across the kitchen carpet sopping up the water, the cupboard had been emptied and wiped out, and the errant joint repaired—thanks to our neighbors, Scott and Julie. Julie, with a preschooler of her own in tow, held the baby. Rachael was smiling. Julie's presence had a calming effect.

Scott and Julie are like that—they'll drop whatever they're doing to lend a helping hand. Last winter when my husband was working long hours, Scott blew the snow out of our lengthy driveway. And when I needed canning lids this fall, Julie gave me three boxes, even though I needed only one and the stores were all out of that size.

Living out in the middle of nowhere like we do, having good neighbors is important.

But what's even more important is *being* a good neighbor. Too often I feel helpless and don't know how—or lack the courage—to respond when someone near has a need. I tell them I'll pray. Prayer is safe. It's not a big commitment of time and energy, and I can do it at my convenience. And I don't have to worry about my offers of help being rejected.

But truly loving your neighbor means putting shoes on those prayers—and sometimes, as in our case, boots.

Thank You, Lord, for neighbors like Scott and Julie. Show me how I, too, can be a good neighbor. Amen.

MORE TEA: Read and reflect on Luke 10:25–37.

The Book of Revelation:

Letters to the Churches

Blessed is he who reads and those who hear the words of this prophecy, and keep those things which are written in it; for the time is near.

–Revelation 1:3 NKJV

Waiting for Alexander

Come, Lord Jesus! –Revelation 22:20 NIV

I'VE NEVER LIKED WAITING, so it's a good thing my first child made his entrance into this world nine days early and I had C-sections for the other two. Even our first grandchild did me a favor and arrived before his due date.

Not so with grandchild number two. My daughter noted she had all the signs of impending labor nearly a month before her actual due date, so we figured Alexander would arrive any time.

Not wanting to miss out on this important milestone in our daughter's life, my husband and I planned to make the twelve-hour trip to Georgia as soon as we got the call that Alexander was on his way. A playpen full of Christmas presents and baby gifts waited in the living room. I fought the urge to move the laundry from the dryer straight to the suitcase.

We made arrangements for time off from work, had all the bills ready to mail, and kept the cell phone battery charged up and the gas tank full. My husband changed the oil, checked the tire pressure, and refilled the windshield washer fluid reservoirs. I kept up-to-date on the weather forecast, flicking on The

Weather Channel several times a day, checking the route we'd take.

Except for the last-minute items, we were ready to go. All we needed was the call. We knew it would come, sooner or later. It wouldn't have done any good, though, to sit by the phone, waiting for it to ring. I still had responsibilities to fulfill. Waiting is hard at times, but it doesn't put life on hold.

Christians are also waiting for an important arrival—the Second Coming of Jesus Christ. Just like with the birth of a baby, it's futile to try to pinpoint when Jesus will return. Jesus Himself said that no one, except God the Father, knows the day or the hour (Matthew 24:36). And just like with Alexander, we are to watch and wait.

But He doesn't expect us to sit around in the meantime. In fact, another definition for wait is "to act as a servant." Until Jesus appears, we are to serve Him by serving others (Matthew 25:31–46): loving, encouraging, sharing, teaching, feeding, clothing, visiting, forgiving, praying.

Just as there was great joy when Alexander finally arrived, there will be great joy for those who are ready and waiting when Jesus returns.

And we know He *will* come sooner or later. Are you ready?

When You return, Lord Jesus, may You find me faithfully doing what You have called me to do. Amen.

MORE TEA: Read and reflect on Luke 12:35–38.

Rekindling the Romance

You have forsaken your first love. –Revelation 2:4 NIV

"WHAT WAS IT THAT attracted you to me when we first met?" I asked my husband. I wasn't fishing for a compliment. I was trying to rekindle the romance.

Marriage, raising children, and the anxieties of daily life have a way of tarnishing the glow of first love. After thirty-two years, we fell into a kind of deadening drudgery: get up, go to work, come home, eat supper, do household chores, shower, go to bed, then wake up to the same old schedule, day in and day out. Our lives are frighteningly similar to the ditty: "I digga the ditch to make the money to buy the food to give me the strength to digga the ditch."

To enjoy a thriving marriage, we're told, we have to keep the romance alive. Hard work when he's snoring on the couch every evening while I fight to keep my eyes open long enough to read the newspaper. Yet the high point of my day is the minute he walks through the door. And I still thrill at the sound of his voice and the twinkle in his eyes.

We just don't take the time to say or do the things that made our relationship flourish nearly three decades ago. He no longer raves about my cooking. I don't make homemade noodles or spaghetti sauce from scratch anymore. He no longer gives the vehicle a thorough cleaning when we go someplace. I stopped taking the time to look my best when he's around. He rarely reads anything I write or tells me about his day; I stopped taking Sunday afternoon walks in the woods with him so I could either take a nap or read a book.

Over time, the "don't do anymore" list grew as we each seemed to retreat into our own, separate shells. Afraid of losing me for us, I became more assertive about my wants and needs, and looked less to his. Small wonder the romance fizzled.

But now that the children are grown and gone, we've taken more time with each other. We've gone shopping—just the two of us—watched a movie in a theater and ate out at a non-fast food restaurant. Slowly we're beginning to share our dreams once again. Getting back to the things we used to do when we were dating seems to be rekindling the romance.

My relationship with my husband is a model of my relationship with God. Just as I need to keep the romance alive in my marriage, so should I keep the flames of love burning for God.

"You do not love me now as you did at first," Jesus told the Ephesian church in Revelation 2:4. Those words reverberate through time and echo in my heart.

How long has it been since I got down on my knees and talked to God from my heart? How long has it been since I gave Him quality time, when my mind is fresh and I'm not worn out from the day's chores? When was the last time I tried to understand what He's telling me in His Word?

I don't doubt for an instant that He loves me unconditionally. It's just that my response to that love needs work. "Think about those times of your first love," Jesus says, "and do the things you did at first" (Rev. 2:5).

With my husband—and with God—I need to remember that it's not the occasional big things, but the little things day after day that keep the romance alive.

Lord, help me to love You with all my heart, soul, and mind. (Matthew 22:37) Amen.

MORE TEA: Read and reflect on Revelation 2:1–7.

Eyes on the Prize

Don't quit. Remain faithful, even when facing death, and I will give you the crown of life. –Revelation 2:10 The Message

IN SEPTEMBER 1979 WE started building our house on the do-it-yourself, pay-as-you-go plan. We avoided a mortgage only because at that time no bank would lend us the money. I couldn't blame them. We were a risk: Only one income supporting a family of three, soon to be four—and that from a job that paid barely enough to keep us above the poverty level. Oh, I could have gone back to teaching, but I wanted to be home with my kids.

Five years after moving into an unfinished basement—mere weeks before our third and youngest child was born—we moved the bedrooms to the second floor. Construction stalled as we ferried our children to ball games, piano lessons, dance recitals and slumber parties. Life was good, even in an unfinished house.

Twenty-six years after we first put the shovel to the soil, we covered the ragged black paper with log siding. A year later we moved the kitchen and dining room upstairs. By then the kids were gone, and grandchildren were popping in.

Over the years, there were hardships and setbacks. At times we despaired of ever getting done, but we never gave up. Our dream was log siding, so we'd tack up drawings of log homes on the inside of a kitchen cupboard door so we'd see it everyday. We researched materials and prices, always believing—knowing—someday we'd reach our goal, and all the work and sacrifice would be worth it.

"Remain faithful even when facing death," Jesus instructed the church at Smyrna, "and I will give you the crown of life."

The church at Smyrna—one of two churches in the Revelation letters that didn't receive criticism—was a persecuted church. Because of their faith, they endured bitter suffering, hardships, and tribulations. They were poor materially, but Jesus told them they were really rich. Although He didn't remove them from the trials, they remained faithful. They knew that on the other side of the persecution was the glory of Heaven, where they would spend eternity.

How have I responded in times of hardship and trouble? Sorry to say, too often I've whined and complained and allowed my faith to falter. But eventually I learned to fix my eyes on the promise of better things to come—Heaven. I realized that everything I have here on earth—even my finished house—is only temporary.

The church at Smyrna, facing death for what they believed, set an example by their unwavering faith. They knew the difference between the temporary and the permanent, and kept their eyes on the prize.

Can we, who have so much more of the world's wealth and so much less persecution, do any less?

Lord, help me to remain steadfast and faithful to You in good times and bad. Remind me to keep my eyes on eternity. Amen.

MORE TEA: Read and reflect on Revelation 2:8–11.

When Smoke Gets in Your Eyes

Religion that God our Father accepts as pure and faultless is this: to look after orphans and widows in their distress and to keep oneself from being polluted by the world. – James 1:27 NIV

MY PARENTS WERE FAIRLY HEAVY smokers, so cigarette smoke permeated everything in the house I grew up in, including our clothes and hair. But I never noticed it because that's what I was used to. Then I went away to college, where cleaner air was the norm. I'll never forget the time I went home for a weekend visit and stopped at a friend's house on the way back to school.

"Whew!" his mother blurted out. "You smell like a smoke stack!"

Perhaps her comment was insensitive, but it made me realize smoking affected not only those who smoked but also those around them.

The longer I stayed away from cigarette smoke, the more sensitive I became when I did come in contact with it. An evening of playing board games with family members who smoked left me with nasal congestion, a sore throat, and watery, burning eyes the next morning. I became so sensitive that even old, stale smoke affected me.

Sin affects us the same way. When we're used to it, it doesn't bother us at all. We may not even see anything wrong with it. Once we chose to follow Jesus, however, we immerse ourselves in a brand new life, studying Scripture, spending time in prayer and fellowship with other believers—and distancing ourselves from the sin that once permeated our lives. We grow in our sensitivity to wrong, and any encounter with it leaves us feeling sick in our souls. It should, anyway.

But perhaps over time we compromise and allow a worldly attitude to drift in, like the church at Pergamum (also called Pergamos), a city "where Satan lived" (Revelation 2:13). Sin and worldliness surrounded these believers, yet they were loyal to Jesus, even in the face of martyrdom.

But clinging to their faith wasn't enough. Jesus expected them to speak out against sin—every single instance of it. Instead, they chose not to make waves and tolerated those who were teaching a false doctrine and were leading people astray.

Am I the same? Do I refuse to make waves when I encounter sin? How do I tolerate compromise with worldliness? In my speech, do I spread gossip, tell white lies, intentionally deceive others, keep silent when God's name is used irreverently? In what I look at: Are the books I read, the shows I watch, and the songs and programs I listen to morally sound? What about my actions? Do I have a what's-in-it-for-me or a what-can-I-do-for-you attitude?

"Do not conform to the pattern of the world," Paul instructs us in Romans 12:2.

"Friendship with the world makes you an enemy of God," James warns (James 4:4 NLT)

Living a holy life in a society permeated with sin isn't easy, but with God's help, we can effect change around us—if we maintain the change within us.

Lord, help me to remain pure in a world that is increasingly getting further from You. Amen.

MORE TEA: Read and reflect on Revelation 2:12–17.

One Bad Apple

Do not be misled: Bad company corrupts good character. –1 Corinthians 15:3 NIV

YOU'VE HEARD THE EXPRESSION, "One bad apple spoils the barrel," but do you know why? Until recently, I never gave it much thought.

Back in my gardening days, I removed overripe, damaged, or rotting fruits and vegetables from their storage container—usually a five-gallon bucket or large cardboard box—until I had enough to warrant a day in the canning kitchen. I assumed bacteria from the decaying produce would contaminate the rest. Not quite.

Actually, fruits and vegetables produce ethylene, a substance that aids in the maturation process. Called the "death" hormone, ethylene is released into the surrounding atmosphere as a gas. The more the fruit ripens, the more ethylene gas is released.

A closed storage container prevents the gas from escaping, allowing it to build up—and be reabsorbed by the stored fruit, which produces even more ethylene, thus hastening the ripening (and death) of the fruit. That's why a tomato ripens more quickly when placed in a closed container, such as paper bag.

And why one rotten apple, by releasing so much ethylene, can cause the rest of the batch, which absorbs it, to spoil.

In the first-century church of Thyatira, the bad apple was a woman whom Jesus referred to as "Jezebel" (Revelation 2:20).

In Thyatira membership in a trade or craft guild was essential if you wanted to succeed in business. The problem was each guild was dedicated to a pagan god. Christian members were caught in a quandary: They knew it was wrong to eat meat sacrificed to these idols, but how could they avoid it and retain membership in an organization that influenced their livelihood? In addition, meetings often turned into drunken orgies.

Their solution was to ride the fence. While they refused to participate in what they knew was wrong, they didn't speak out against it, either. And when "Jezebel," a self-proclaimed prophetess, insisted that it was okay to tolerate and even to participate in these pagan practices, they didn't challenge her. It was better to play it safe.

Their lack of courage resulted in believers being led astray and a stern warning of judgment to come if they didn't get off the fence.

Are we any better today? We may commend ourselves for our faith, service, and spiritual growth, but do we refuse to speak out against something or someone we know is wrong? Do we shy away from being the lone voice objecting because we're afraid of what people will say? Do we justify our cowardice with excuses?

Confronting sin, especially popular sin, requires courage, faith, and risk. We risk our reputation, our popularity, and sometimes, as in the case of the believers in Thyatira, our finances.

But Jesus doesn't commend us for playing it safe. He demands obedience, and obedience requires confronting the sin and the sinner.

Where do you need to get off the fence and deal with the rotten apple before the whole bunch is spoiled?

Lord, give me the courage to confront wrong and the grace to confront the wrongdoer in love. Amen.

MORE TEA: Read and reflect on Revelation 2:18–29.

The Heart of the Matter

Man looks at the outward appearance, but the LORD looks at the heart. –1 Samuel 16:7 NIV

I WAS EXCITED: MOM and Dad were making plans to put new siding on our house. As a teenager, I wanted to fit in, and our old-fashioned wood siding just didn't cut it. While my parents explored the options, I imagined what our house would look like with new, white aluminum siding—the latest trend. Now that would definitely put me up a few notches on the teen scene.

But, alas, I was to remain in my lowly status because my parents decided to tear off the old siding and replace it with new wood siding identical to what was removed. I tried to talk them out of it.

"Aluminum siding would be a lot quicker because it's put on right over the old stuff," I argued.

"Oh, no," Mom objected. "I won't cover up all that dirt and rotten wood. Yuck! I couldn't live in a house knowing all that filth was under there."

The church at Sardis had the same problem I had: thinking a nice cover was all that was needed, when underneath was decay.

On the outside, they looked, talked, and acted like Christians, but on the inside they weren't real believers. They were merely playing at Christianity, meaninglessly going through the motions. Jesus, who knew their hearts, saw right through their hypocrisy.

"You have a reputation for being alive," He told them, "but you are dead."

Jerry Jenkins, author of the bestselling Left Behind series, tells of a time when, as a teenage counselor at a Christian summer youth camp, he was confronted with his own hypocrisy.

Raised in a devout Christian home, he loved everything about church and Sunday school and was "one of those teenagers who had never been in trouble." But he refrained from sharing his faith with his friends at school because "he didn't want to push his beliefs on anyone."

Then one day at camp the speaker for the evening service asked Jerry what he should speak about.

"Well," Jerry said, "there are a lot of phonies here. Maybe something on really being what you say you are all the time."

That evening, the speaker addressed the topic Jerry suggested. At first he sat there, mentally patting himself on the back for doing all the right things and avoiding all the wrong things. But then the speaker's words began to pierce his heart.

"Maybe you're not doing anything wrong. Maybe you think you're okay with the Lord," the speaker said. "But do your friends even know you're a believer? Or are you a secret-service Christian, saving your piety for Sundays and home?"

Jerry was the first on his feet when the speaker was done. He'd seen himself as one of those phonies he himself referred to.

The remedy for a spiritual coma, Jesus said, is to wake up and get moving in the right direction for the right reasons. Christianity is more than an outward show to impress others. It's obeying God out of a heart of love.

Create in me a clean heart, O God, and renew a right spirit within me so that I can stay alive and thrive spiritually. Amen.

MORE TEA: Read and reflect on Revelation 3:1–6.

O Me of Little Faith

I have set before you an open door. –Revelation 3:8 RSV

TEACHING IS MY PASSION. So when God opened the door to a teaching position in 2001, I enthusiastically ran through. For four years I thanked God every day for granting me my heart's desire.

Then one year prior to the start of school I sensed God calling me to relinquish the job I loved.

How can this be? I wondered.

The more I prayed, the stronger I felt I was to resign and focus on freelance writing. But I hedged. I procrastinated. I reasoned. I justified my refusal to obey. My meager teaching income (I worked in a private, Christian school) was at least steady, but the sparse pay for freelance writing was sporadic, unless you're Max Lucado. Trusting God to provide was more than I was comfortable with. "Walk by sight, not by faith" was my motto. Besides, how did I know for sure this was God speaking?

The crisis passed a few weeks into the first semester, but I endured a miserable year. The joy disappeared. A mysterious physical malady plagued me. The constant wrestling with doubt and fear left me drained physically, mentally, emotionally, and spiritually.

Then, in a surprising (for me) and awesome answer to prayer, God provided the means to attend a writers' conference the following summer. The trip was a turning point. Two weeks after my return, I submitted my resignation although I had no book contract or writing assignment. The burden of doubt lifted, the angst of anxiety dissipated, and, for the first time in a year, I felt free. Peace and joy flooded my soul.

Would God provide? I believed He would. I didn't know how, but I didn't think He wanted me to know. I was, instead, to walk by faith, not by sight (2 Corinthians 5:7).

There were times I was tempted to focus on my fears. So I posted a quote by D.L. Moody on my work station where I could see it every day: "Do not doubt in the dark what God has shown you in the light."

I believed God would bless me for my obedience, but my definition of blessing changed: His presence day by day, moment by moment, was blessing enough (Exodus 33:14; Hebrews 13:5). Knowing that *El Shaddai* keeps His word was blessing enough (Titus 1:2).

I wasn't promised success, but, again, God's meaning of the word was not the same as mine. While I equated success with outcome—my writing achievements—God was more concerned with process: teaching me to obey, moment by moment, day by day. For that's how He transforms me from the inside out. "God has not called me to be successful," Mother Teresa once said. "He has called me to be faithful."

I thought it would take strong faith for me to step through the door God had opened, but I was wrong. The church in Philadelphia had but "little strength," yet they obeyed God. "I know all the things you do," Jesus told them, "and I have opened a door for you that no one can shut" (Revelation 3:8).

Obedience doesn't require a ton of faith—just enough to take the next step through the door that He has opened.

Grant me wisdom, dear Lord, to recognize a door You have opened and the courage to go through—without hesitation. Amen.

MORE TEA: Read and reflect on Revelation 3:7–13.

Cookie Monster

Why do you spend money for what is not bread, and your wages for what does not satisfy? Listen carefully to Me, and eat what is good, and let your soul delight itself in abundance. – Isaiah 55:2 NKJV

I DON'T BAKE COOKIES anymore. Not even for holidays. Why? Because I'll eat them for breakfast. I'll eat them for lunch. I'll eat them for my mid-afternoon and bedtime snacks. The more I eat, the more I want.

My husband, on the other hand, knows when to say when. He stores the cookies we buy for his snacks high on a shelf in a kitchen cupboard—high enough so that I can't reach them on tiptoe, but he can because he's six-foot-thee. Most of the time that's enough to stop me from playing cookie monster. Note I said, "most of the time." For those occasions when I hear those sweet little round things calling my name, I keep a small stool in the kitchen that's just the right height for me to pilfer a half dozen or so to dip in my coffee. Do that too close to suppertime, though, and I'm not hungry for the food that will satisfy my body's real needs.

In His final letter to the first century churches, Jesus warned the affluent Laodicean church that they, too, were filling up on things that didn't satisfy their real need: "You say, 'I am rich. I have everything I want. I don't need a thing!' And you don't realize that you are wretched and miserable and poor and blind and naked" (Revelation 3:17).

Their wealth was like cookies: Junk food with little, if any, nutritional value. It filled them up with self-sufficiency so that they were no longer hungry for God. As a result, they were lukewarm Christians— unenthusiastic, half-hearted, unexcited, indifferent—doing just enough, they thought, to get by. And lukewarm is nauseating. Ever drink a glass of lukewarm water on a hot day?

But are we any different than the Laodiceans? Most of us in America have all we need. We have so much that our attics and garages overflow into rented storage bins. Yet look at our credit card debt. You'd think our motto was "In goods we trust." Yet what is our spiritual condition? Do we have the form of religion but lack true spiritual power? (2 Timothy 3:5)

The remedy, Jesus said, is to obtain our riches from Him—riches that satisfy for all eternity (Matthew 6:19–21). We do that by putting Him first in every aspect of our lives (Matthew 6:33). We do it by obedience. We do it by praying and reading His Word and putting it into practice. We do it by serving others.

For if we have God—and He has us—then we have everything we need. And who knows? Maybe there will be a few cookies thrown in.

Oh, God, send us the Holy Spirit! Give us both the breath of spiritual life and the fire of unconquerable zeal. You are our God ... The Kingdom comes not, and the work is flagging. Oh, that You would send the wind and the fire! And You will do this when we are all in one accord, all believing, all expecting, all prepared by prayer. Amen. (Charles Haddon Spurgeon)

MORE TEA: Read and reflect on Revelation 3:14–22.

The Ten Commandments

Blessed are they whose way is blameless,
who walk according to the law of the LORD.
Blessed are they who keep his statutes
and seek him with all their heart.

–Psalm 119: 1 NIV

The Ten Commandments

I. "I am the Lord thy God."

II. "Thou shalt not have any strange gods before Me."

III. "Thou shalt not take the name of the Lord thy God in vain."

IV. "Remember to keep holy the Sabbath day."

V. "Honor thy father and mother."

VI. "Thou shalt not kill."

VII. "Thou shalt not commit adultery."

VIII. "Thou shalt not steal."

IX. "Thou shalt not bear false witness against thy neighbor."

X. "Thou shalt not covet."

Finding My Way

Direct my footsteps according to your word; let no sin rule over me. –Psalm 119:133 NIV

WHEN I WAS ABOUT ten or eleven years old and my family was vacationing at our cabin in the mountains of western Pennsylvania, my sister and I decided to take a walk in the woods. We walked, all right, and walked and walked and walked—because we couldn't find our way back to the cabin!

I remember walking through the same meadow about three times. Finally, after what seemed like hours, we saw the outline of a building through the trees. At last! Camp! As we got closer, however, we realized that it wasn't our cabin at all nor any of the three cabins near ours but a rustic log cabin we hadn't seen before. Where were we?

A boy about my age was chopping wood in the backyard. As we approached, he turned to leave, apparently not hearing us.

"Stop! Stop!" we cried, breaking into a run, hopping over fallen limbs and pushing through waist-high grass. "We're lost! Stop!"

It turned out that we had wandered in the opposite direction of our cabin. Neither I nor my sister even knew what direction camp was. We just followed the way through the woods that was easiest and seemed to lead us in the direction we wanted to go. We didn't have a compass, but it wouldn't have done us much good because neither one of us knew how to use one.

A compass helps the traveler because its needle always points north. But before you can make use of a compass, you need to know three things: where you want to go, where you are now and what direction—north, south, east or west—to travel. Once you know that, you can set out, using the compass to keep on course.

As we travel through life, we need a compass to guide us. There are many paths we can take, some seeming to lead us in the way we want to go but, in reality, will take us in the opposite direction. God knew we needed help, so He gave us His Word. He began by writing, with His own hand, ten simple laws that, if we follow them, will lead us to a fulfilling, satisfying life.

The Ten Commandments. Like a cross, with a vertical beam and a horizontal one, these ten rules govern all our relationships. The first four deal with our relationship with God (the vertical beam); the last six with our relationships with others (the horizontal beam).

The Ten Commandments. The subject of Hollywood movies and lawsuits. Why have they become so controversial? And how do laws established 3,450 years ago relate to us today?

This series delves into each commandment. One commandment per reading. Study it, meditate on it, and explore its relevance to today's world and your life. Let the Holy Spirit be your teacher.

As we study the Decalogue, as the Ten Commandments are sometimes called, you'll notice the suggested readings will be from Psalm 119, a psalm written as a devotional on God's Word.

Like a compass, God's Word points us in the direction we are to go. But we first need to find out where we are: on the narrow path that leads to life or the broad way that leads to eternal death (Matthew 7:13–14). Only then can we set our course for true north: God Himself.

"Blessed are they whose way is blameless, who walk according to the law of the LORD. Blessed are they who keep his statutes and seek him with all their heart." – Psalm 119:1 NIV

Come, Holy Spirit, be my teacher and our guide as I make my way through a cluttered, loud world where there is so much to lure me away from the only path that leads to everlasting life. Give me wisdom to understand God's Word, the faith to believe it, and the courage to obey it. Amen.

MORE TEA: Read and reflect on Psalm 119:1–16; Exodus 20:1–17.

Cat or Dog?

"I am the LORD your God." –Exodus 20:2 NKJV

The fear of the LORD is the beginning of wisdom, and knowledge of the Holy One is understanding. – Proverbs 9:10 NIV

A NEWSPAPER AD LEFT me chuckling: "Free to good home: Litter-trained kittens." I understood the intent: whoever wanted a kitten wouldn't have to worry about training it to use the litter box. But anyone with experience knows you can't train a cat. A cat does what it darn well pleases.

Case in point: When my daughter obtained two kittens from the local humane society, she kept squirt guns around the house to keep them off the countertops and tables. Whenever the felines trespassed on forbidden territory, she'd shoot a jet of water toward them. It didn't work. As for litter training, all I did with my kittens was plop them in the litter box once or twice. They instinctively knew what to do.

We had a cat in our home for thirty years. I never needed to train one in the way I wanted it to go. Rather, it seemed the cat trained me. When she wanted out, she'd go to the door and meow. When she wanted back in, she'd peer in one of the windows, and, if I didn't come right away, tap on the glass with her claws.

Our dog, on the other hand, was an entirely different story. It takes time and patience to train a canine, but eventually you can command it to roll over, give you a paw, fetch a ball, heel, come, and stay. The dog learns who the master is—the person who takes care of its needs and is to be obeyed. You can take care of a cat's needs all you want, but it will never accept you as master. Sometimes I think it's the other way around. But a dog, once you've established the relationship, will be devoted, loyal, and faithful, even mourning the master's death.

When it comes to us, we humans have a problem with the word *master*. We're like cats—we want to master rather than be mastered. We want our independence to be who we want to be and do what we want to do. We want to be masters of our own destiny.

Such a creed may be lofty, idealistic, inspirational, and motivational, but it isn't biblical. And the Bible is our guidebook for living, our manufacturer's handbook. And embedded in the pages of Scripture are ten simple rules that govern our relationships, first with God, then with others.

The very first commandment establishes the primary relationship and sets the foundation for the other nine: God tell us who He is and what He's done for us:

"I am the LORD your God, who brought you out of Egypt, out of the land of slavery. You shall have no other gods before me" (Exodus 20:2–3).

Who *is* God? He is LORD. The word *LORD* (all capital letters) is translated from the Hebrew word *Yahweh* (YHWH), which means the self-existent or Eternal One, the One who exists because of who He is. The word *Lord* (Hebrew *Adonai*), when used for God, means "master or owner of all things.

Each of us must find out for ourselves the identity of our master.

Look around. Read the headlines. Listen to and watch the news. It's like the familiar adage, too many cooks spoil the soup. Too many masters spoil the world, society as a whole. No wonder we have problems with the other nine commandments: We don't have God in His rightful place.

There can be only one master. Either it's self or God. Which one created the universe? Which one is omnipotent, omniscient, omnipresent, all-wise, eternal, faithful, good, merciful, just, and holy? Which one takes care of our needs and, hence, is to be obeyed? Which one suffered a horrific death to break the bonds of our slavery to sin and open the way to our Promised Land—Heaven? Isn't that the Master we should heed?

How about you: Are you a cat or a dog?

"Let him who boasts, boast about this: that he understands and knows Me, that I am the LORD, who exercises kindness, justice and righteousness on earth, for in these I delight, declares the LORD" (Jeremiah 9:24).

Dear God, when I am tempted to put myself on the throne instead of You, remind me of Who You are—Elohim, Yahweh, Adonai—*and of what I am and how foolish that would be. Amen.*

MORE TEA:

Read and reflect on Psalm 119:17–22; Exodus 20:1–17.

I Will Not Bow Down

"You shall not make for yourself an idol in the form of anything in the heaven above or on the earth beneath or in the waters below. You shall not bow down to them or worship them" –Exodus 20:4–5 NIV.

For all the gods of the nations are idols, but the LORD made the heavens. – Psalm 96:5 NIV

WHEN I WAS IN college, one of the girls in my dormitory claimed to be able to foretell someone's future by reading the lines in that person's palms. Of course, I had her read my palm.

"You're going to get married and have four boys," she told me.

I raised two sons and a daughter.

Who isn't curious about the future? Who doesn't want to know what the coming days and years have in store? In high school, a group of us got together one Friday evening and played with a Ouiji board. We were just looking to have some fun. We were clueless that we were on dangerous ground, dabbling in the occult.

The occult—practices used to seek supernatural knowledge and power—is expressly forbidden by God Himself: "Let no one be found among you … who practices divination or sorcery, interprets omens, engages in witchcraft or casts spells, or who is a medium or spiritist or who consults the dead. Anyone who does these things is detestable to the LORD" (Deuteronomy 18:10–12). Why? Because this supernatural power and knowledge doesn't come from God. It comes from His archenemy: Satan and his demons.

Today we don't have to look very far to find those who claim to be able to foretell the future. The means they profess to use are many: tarot cards, psychic ability, the stars, seances. They hang out their shingles or advertise their wares on television. Witchcraft and sorcery are the themes of many a television show or movie, even on children's networks.

Consulting the stars to foretell the future is to bypass the Maker of the stars—the omnipotent, omniscient, omnipresent, eternal, infinite, immutable, sovereign, holy, one and only God. And the second commandment forbids us to worship anything but God.

You may not dabble in the occult, but there are other ways God gets nudged out of first place. Matthew Henry, the renowned Bible commentator, gave us insight into how this can happen:

"Pride makes a god of self, covetousness makes a god of money, sensuality makes a god of the belly; whatever is esteemed or loved, feared or served, delighted in or depended on, more than God, that (whatever it is) we do in effect make a god of."

I may not bow down physically to an idol, but whenever I put anything before God, I am worshipping that thing by giving honor and reverence to it that belongs only to God. I need to examine my life daily and ask God to show me the idols that have crept into my life.

I need to know Him better, love Him more, and serve Him with every thought, word and deed, because the closer I get to God, the more I realize that He and He alone, controls the future, and He and He alone is worthy of my total praise and adoration.

"Their idols are silver and gold, made by the hands of men. They have mouths, but cannot speak, eyes, but they cannot see; they have ears, but cannot hear, noses, but they cannot smell; they have hands, but they cannot feel, feet, but they cannot walk; nor can they utter a sound with their throats. Those who make them will be like them, and so will all who trust in them" (Psalm 115:4–8 NIV).

You alone, O God, do I worship. Amen.

MORE TEA: Read and reflect on Exodus 20:4–6; Psalm 115.

Hallowed Be Thy Name

You shall not misuse the name of the LORD your God. – Exodus 20:7 NIV

WHEN MY SON AND his friends were in high school and a part of our church's youth group, they'd really get into the worship music.

One song especially seemed to be a favorite: "Blessed Be the Name of the Lord." When we'd come to the part where we sang the words of Proverbs 18:10—"The name of the LORD is a strong tower; the righteous run to it and are safe"—they'd have the entire church doing the motions with the words: flexing triceps for "strong;" forming a tower with two arms raised above the head, hands together at the fingertips; running in place ("run into it"); and, of course, a baseball umpire's motion when a player is safe.

The motions reinforce the words and make them easier to remember. And quite a number of folks, especially those with too much on their minds or those whose years are creeping up on them (and I fall into both categories), need some help remembering things, especially names.

God's name isn't hard to remember, though. I hear it around me everyday, often in ways that give no honor to the name that the Jews considered so holy, they wouldn't even pronounce it or write it out entirely: YHWH. The first line of the Lord's Prayer reinforces the holiness of God's name: "Our Father in Heaven, hallowed be Your name" (Matthew 6:9). The word "hallowed" means "to make or consider holy or sacred; to honor as holy or sacred."

Little, if anything, in our society today is even considered holy, let alone God's name. The word itself conjures up visions of pious saints, perfect in all they said and did. This, of course, is false. Only one Person who ever walked this unholy ground we call earth was ever perfect—Jesus Christ, the only begotten Son of God, the second Person of the Trinity. The rest of us struggle with our human nature.

God's holiness is something we humans cannot fathom. When the prophet Isaiah saw the vision of God seated on His throne (Isaiah 6:1–7), and angels surrounding Him calling, "Holy, holy, holy is the LORD Almighty," he immediately felt his sinfulness.

"Woe is me!" Isaiah cried. "I am a man of unclean lips, and I live among a people of unclean lips, and my eyes have seen the King, the LORD Almighty."

Centuries later, the apostle Peter, after a night of fruitless fishing, obeyed Jesus and let down his nets one more time—for the catch of a lifetime. Falling at Jesus' feet, Peter cried, "Go away from me, Lord; I am a sinful man!" (Luke 5:8 NIV)

Both Moses and Joshua, when approaching the Holy, were told to "take off your sandals, for place where you are standing is holy ground" (Exodus 3:5; Joshua 5:15).

Job's reaction, after God responded to his complaints about the unfairness of his troubles, after catching a glimpse of the Holy, was to cry, "Surely I spoke of things I did not understand, things too wonderful for me to know … My ears had heard of you, but now my eyes have seen you. Therefore I despise myself and repent in dust and ashes" (Job 42:3,5–6 NIV).

How do we react today when we are given glimpses into God's holiness? Like Job, Moses, Joshua, Isaiah, and Peter, are we made painfully aware of our sinfulness, of our unworthiness? Or do we walk away, allowing the glow of the Holy in our hearts and lives to fade when we go out into a world where nothing is truly holy?

"Let those who love Your name Be joyful in You." –Psalm 5:11 NKJV

Too many times, O LORD, I hear Your holy name used flippantly. Forgive me when I, too, take Your name, and all it means, lightly. Teach me what holy means. Amen.

MORE TEA: Read and reflect on Isaiah 6:1–7; Psalm 119:33–48.

My Day of Rest

"Remember the Sabbath day, by keeping it holy." –Exodus 20:8 NKJV

He makes me lie down in green pastures, he leads me beside quiet waters, he restores my soul. –Psalm 23:2–3 NIV

IT'S FUNNY HOW SONGS from childhood stay with us throughout life. I remember my mother singing along with the songs that blasted from the radio that sat atop the refrigerator as she went about her housework. Singing made the work seem easier, the time go by faster, and lightened the load of responsibility, care, and worry.

I especially remember one song that even I liked to sing—"Never on a Sunday." Nearly sixty years later I still find myself quietly singing the lyrics, especially when Sunday has become anything but a day of rest. When I was a child, Sundays meant reading the comics (we called them the "funnies"), going to church, having a sit-down dinner of roast beef with the entire family, and relaxing the rest of the day.

I remember when I first became aware of the increased pace of life on Sundays. We live in the country, and for years we attended a small country church near our home and rarely had a reason to come to town on a Sunday. One Sunday we came to town to bring my daughter's friend, who had spent the weekend with us, home. Town was even busier, I thought, than a weekday. Cars were buzzing down the main street, blocking intersections, and jumping red lights, all in a hurry to get where they were going. Parking lots were full.

Whatever happened to Sunday being a day of rest? I wondered.

Modern technology has given us devices that save time and labor, but what do we do with the time we save? Cram more activities into already over-crowded schedules. Stress has become a major health issue.

When I worked outside the home putting in a forty-plus-hour work week, I found myself tempted to use Sunday as an extra Saturday. I lived my life like I drove: hurried, tail-gating slow pokes, jumping red lights, slowing down and cruising through stop signs. I have to remind myself that stop means exactly that. It doesn't mean merge or yield.

And that's what Sabbath literally means. Sabbath comes from a Hebrew word meaning "to stop or to rest from work." God Himself set the example: "By the seventh day God had finished the work he had been doing; so on the seventh day he rested from all his work. And God blessed the seventh day and made it holy, because on it he rested from all the work of creating that he had done" (Genesis 2:2–3 NIV).

Holy in this case means "set apart for special use." No other day was blessed, only Sunday. No other day was set apart, only

Sunday. Sunday was not meant to be a burden, but a time of laying aside the burdens and focusing on rest and worship.

Sunday was and is a gift—a gift of time. Time for restoration, time for re-energizing rundown, worn-out bodies and spirits, time to focus on all that God is and does, and worship Him. And true worship, like singing, will make work the rest of the week seem easier and the burdens we carry lighter.

Help me, Lord, to put away the ever-present do-list on Sunday and take that nap, because I know I will feel better the rest of the week. Amen.

MORE TEA:

Read and reflect on Exodus 20:8–11; Psalm 119:49–64.

Generation Gap

Honor your father and your mother, so that you may live long in the land the LORD your God is giving you. –Exodus 20:12 NIV

"Honor your father and your mother"—which is the first commandment with a promise—that it may go well with you and that you may enjoy long life on earth. –Ephesians 6:2–3 NIV

GROWING UP IN THE 1950s and sixties, I understood the fifth commandment, "Honor your father and your mother," to mean to obey and respect them, not to talk back to them or make fun of them. But honor means more than that. It also means to cherish, to prize highly, to treat as precious and valuable.

Like most kids, though, I didn't appreciate my parents until I became a parent myself. Then it was too late. Dad died when I was twenty, and Mom suffered from Alzheimer's disease until she died fifteen years later.

My parents' generation fought World War II and the Korean War. Many didn't even finish high school because they wanted to do their part. After the war, they married, raised families, supported their churches, and built communities.

My generation fought a war, too—the Vietnam War. Some of us lost our lives and our loves over there. Those who returned, returned to a nation in tumult: abortion on demand, assassinations, riots. They returned to war protesters, flag burners, draft dodgers, and Hollywood actresses siding with the enemy and making them feel ashamed for doing their part. They returned to flower power that was little more than a façade for crumbling values and moral decay.

So where are we with "honor your father and mother" today, now that we of the flower power generation are of retiring age? Forbidding prayer in schools was only the beginning. Now, headed by the media, the government, and lawyers who claim to fight for what they call civil liberties, society is doing its best to stamp out any reminder of God.

The greatest empires in history were not conquered from without, but crumbled from within. And it all started with moral decay. How do we reverse this downward slide? It all comes back to the fifth commandment, which Paul explained to the Ephesians: "Honor your father and your mother"—which is the first commandment with a promise—*that it may go well with you and that you may enjoy long life on earth*" (Ephesians 6:2–3 NIV, emphasis mine).

The first commandment established the ultimate authority: God. The fifth commandment established authority in the home. There's nothing said of government in the rest of the commandments. No other laws but to love God with all your heart, soul, mind and strength, and to love others as yourself (Matthew 22:36–40).

Fourteen hundred years after God gave the Ten Commandments on Mount Sinai, the apostle Paul described the last days: "There will be terrible times in the last days. People will be lovers of themselves, lovers of money, boastful, proud, abusive, disobedient to their parents, ungrateful, unholy, without love, unforgiving, slanderous, without self-control, brutal, not lovers of the good, treacherous, rash, conceited, lovers of pleasure rather than lovers of God—having a form of godliness but denying its power" (2 Timothy 3:1–5 NIV).

Where did this all start? One Bible commentator wrote, in commenting on the fifth commandment, "Not only in Israel, but in all nations and individual lives, the destruction of the home marks the beginning of the end" (*The Wycliffe Bible Commentary*).

So how to reverse the trend? It all starts in the home. First, put God where He belongs—in first place. Then build strong homes founded on God's Word, honoring our parents, and teaching the next generation to respect the authority God Himself established.

"A wise son brings joy to his father, but a foolish son grief to his mother." –Proverbs 10:1 NIV

Father, when I look at the world around me, I feel only despair. How far we've come from what You planned for us to be! Help us to get our lives back in line with Your Word. Amen.

MORE TEA:

Read and reflect on Proverbs 23:22–25; Psalm 119:65–80.

Murder by Mouth

You shall not murder. –Exodus 20:13 NIV

Let everything you say be good and helpful, so that your words will be an encouragement to those who hear them. – Ephesians 4:29 NLT

MOST OF THE MEMORIES of my college days are not ones I remember with fondness. I learned some hard lessons of life during those pressure-filled academic years.

One incident in particular I still recall with pain. My friends and I had planned a surprise birthday party on our dormitory floor for our friend, Penny. Since we had to wait for her to return from some contrived errand, I decided to spend a few quiet moments with my boyfriend in the downstairs social room.

About the time Penny was to have come back, Tammy, one of the party planners, approached me.

"Penny isn't back yet," she said, "but I'll let you know as soon as she comes."

Then she went upstairs and told the girls, including Penny, who *had* returned, that I said I didn't want to come. After that I had no friends.

Murder by mouth. With her lie, Tammy destroyed precious friendships, my reputation, and what little joy I found in college.

The tongue, James wrote, "is a small thing, but what enormous damage it can do. … It is full of wickedness" that can ruin your whole life. "It is evil and uncontrollable, full of deadly poison" (James 3:5–8).

The tongue is sharper than any knife, slicing into the aorta of someone's character with malicious gossip and causing a reputation to bleed to death. And we hone our skills of verbal cruelty. Maybe that story we're repeating *is* true, however unkind. But does it build up or tear down?

"With his mouth," the writer of Proverbs notes, "the godless destroys his neighbor" (Proverbs 11:9 NIV).

But lies, slander, and gossip aren't the only ways we murder with our mouths. We are adept at destroying dreams, too.

We tell our kids to aim for the stars, then shoot them down when they do. A high school athlete dreams of being a major league ballplayer. A young girl aspires to be an astronaut. A want-to-be writer wrestles with putting a sentence together. A learning- disabled student dreams of becoming a teacher. Do we support them in their pursuits, unlikely as their dreams may seem to us? Or do we "bring them down to reality" with words that are meant to soften the landing?

Who knows, maybe that aspiring ballplayer will be the one in ten thousand who will make it to the big leagues. Perhaps that young woman will walk on the moon someday or discover another star. Or that aspiring writer will win a Pulitzer Prize.

And the student who struggles will become the best teacher because he understands and knows how to help.

Words can kill joy, too. Have you ever said something to someone and watched the light die out of their eyes? Maybe your husband did the laundry and you complain that the clothes aren't folded right. Or perhaps your daughter cleaned the kitchen or your son washed your car, and instead of telling them you appreciate their efforts, you find the places they missed. Or maybe your wife went out of her way and took time, in spite of a busy schedule, to cook your favorite meal of roast beef with homemade noodles, mashed potatoes, and real gravy, and you comment that the meat is a little tough.

"Do to others what you would have them do to you," Jesus commanded us (Matthew 7:12 NIV). That includes our speech: Say to others what you would have them say to you. Framing our words in a positive manner means applying the Philippians 4:8 rule to our speech: Say only the words that are true, noble, right, pure, lovely, admirable, excellent, and praiseworthy.

Words can bring death or life. The choice is ours.

Set a guard, O Lord, over my mouth. Keep watch over the door of my lips Psalm 141:3 NKJV). Amen.

MORE TEA: Read and reflect on James 3:2–12; Psalm 119:81–96.

Stay or Stray?

You shall not commit adultery. – Exodus 20:14 NIV

Let marriage be held in honor among all, and let the marriage bed be undefiled. – Hebrews 13:4 RSV

HIPPIE WANNA-BE THAT I was in the early 1970s, I still chose the traditional wedding vows: "To have and to hold; for better or worse; for richer, for poorer; in sickness and health; to love and to cherish; forsaking all others, till death do us part."

On that day my heart focused on the "better, richer, health" part of that promise. After all, doesn't true love conquer all? Three years later our first child was born, and romance turned to reality. For the next twenty years, we struggled with raising three children on one income, building a house, and the usual battles with life. The better became worse, richer became poorer, and, while our general health remained good, our bodies began to remind us that we weren't getting any younger.

Then, twenty-three years after saying "I do," I ran away from home. There were other factors in my decision to flee to my brother and his wife in Alabama, but my intention was not just a casual visit: I asked him if I could live with him. He responded by purchasing a two-way plane ticket for a nine-day stay.

The morning before I left, I asked my husband to pray with me. In the predawn darkness, we knelt before the love seat in the living room, and I wrapped my arms around him. I visualized holding our relationship, like a wounded, broken bird, in my cupped hands and raising it up to heaven.

"Lord," I prayed silently, "I've done my best, but things just keep getting worse. Make it better. Please. I give it all to You. I don't know what else to do."

There were no issues such as addiction, unfaithfulness, or abuse. It was simply that there seemed to be nothing left—no love, only heartache, disappointment, and frustration. We never talked heart to heart.

I spent the next nine days praying, reading, and searching for answers.

"God will make a way, where there seems to be no way," my brother told me before I returned home.

Seven years later my husband and I knelt before God again. This time it was in church, as his request.

"Let's go up and thank God for our relationship," he whispered to me during the altar call.

As we prayed together, his arm wrapped around me, I remembered that dark morning when I didn't think there was anything left. There was: God. Through His power we were able to work through the issues that threatened our marriage.

Not that things are hunky dory, even now, during the empty nest years and we have time for each other. At times we're like a couple of quirky, squirrelly old folks. But we've learned that love is not only a feeling. It's often an act of the will.

What happens when passion ebbs, our bodies begin to break down, and the hormones dry up? Modern society would have us believe that we can find fulfillment in pills, watching porn, sleeping around. But that's not what God's Word says.

"Honor your marriage and its vows, and remain faithful to one another, guarding the sacredness of sexual intimacy between wife and husband" (Hebrews 13:4 LB, MESSAGE). Honor means to prize highly, to cherish, to show respect for, to treat as precious and valuable.

From the romance stage to the reality stage to the revival stage, marriage is a choice, not a fairy tale. If we commit ourselves unselfishly to our spouses, love them as Christ loves His Bride, the Church (sacrificially), then we won't be tempted to stray. But, instead, with God's help, stay and make our marriages all they can be.

Bless our marriage, Lord. Help us to resolve the issues that threaten our commitment to each other. Amen.

MORE TEA:

Read and reflect on Ephesians 5:21–33; Psalm 119:97–112.

Pickings without Paying

You shall not steal. –Exodus 20:15 NIV

Let the thief no longer steal, but rather let him labor, doing honest work with his own hands, so that he may have something to share with anyone in need. –Ephesians 4:28 ESV

ONE SUMMER DAY WHEN I was a child, my sister and I decided to pick some cherries. So we hiked to the nearest tree and spent the afternoon in its lofty, laden branches, filling our containers with delicious, sweet cherries. The problem was the tree was in a neighbor's yard.

When my mother spied the fruit of our labors, we got called on the carpet.

"Where did these cherries come from?" she asked.

We told her.

"Did you ask permission first?"

"No. We thought since she lives alone, and there were more cherries on the tree than she could ever use, we'd just take some. She wouldn't miss them."

"Taking something that belongs to someone else without asking permission is wrong," my mother explained. "You'll have to go and tell her what you've done and pay for what you took."

Fortunately, the neighbor was understanding and let us keep our pickings without paying.

Stealing infiltrates our daily lives without us even realizing it. We've been programmed to take what we think we deserve. We come up with a thousand reasons why we should have what we want. We justify wrong by convincing ourselves that it's right. We redefine terms to our own selfish advantage.

But whitewashing it doesn't change it. Stealing—no matter the reason, no matter that what we stole was, in our opinion, insignificant—is sin, and sin is an impenetrable wall that separates us from God.

"But I just 'borrowed' it. I was planning to return it," we reason. Borrowing is fine if we ask permission first. While we're borrowing it, we're robbing the owner of the opportunity to use what is his. What happens if what we borrow gets lost, stolen, or broken? Then it's our responsibility to fix it, replace it, or pay for it. And we're not to be cheap in making restitution, either.

In the Old Testament, if a man let his livestock stray into another man's field or vineyard, then he was to make restitution from the best of his own field or vineyard. If a man stole one animal, he was to pay the owner back with five (Exodus 22:1).

In the New Testament, the rich tax collector Zaccheaus told Jesus, "If I have cheated anybody out of anything, I will pay back four times the amount" (Luke 19:8 NIV). We are not to be cheap in making restitution. We are to repay with generosity and quality, even if it means we must sacrifice.

Material possessions and money aren't the only things we can pilfer. We can purloin another person's time, ideas, and words.

Stealing not only means taking something that doesn't belong to us, it also means not giving someone what is due him. We rob God when we don't give Him back a tenth of what He's given us (Malachi 3:8–10). We steal from the government when we don't report all our income on our tax returns. We steal from merchants when we don't return the extra change we've received by mistake. We steal from nonprofit organizations when we don't honor our pledges.

But stealing is a symptom of something more serious. It is an outward manifestation of an inward ailment, and we can't fix the symptoms until we cure the cause. In order to stop our thievery, then, we need to examine our hearts and ask God to remove the reasons, which include selfishness, greed, discontent, covetousness, and envy (Matthew 15:19). And then ask Him to give us a generous and contented heart, for as we think in our hearts, so are we (Proverbs 23:7; Philippians 4:8).

Give me neither poverty nor riches. Give me just enough to satisfy my needs. For, if I grow rich, I may become content without You. And if I am too poor, I may steal, and thus insult Your holy name. Amen. (Proverbs 30:8–9 LB)

MORE TEA:

Read and reflect on Exodus 22:1–15; Psalm 119:112–128.

The Power of Truth

You shall not bear false witness against your neighbor. –Exodus 20:16 NKJV

Stand firm then, with the belt of truth buckled around your waist." –Ephesians 6:13–14 NIV

WE WERE DRIVING BACK to Pennsylvania after a visit with our daughter in South Carolina when it happened. A red pickup truck came rolling off the on-ramp, crossed two lanes of traffic on the interstate highway, and cut right in front of us. My husband swerved left to avoid a collision, but then we were headed for the concrete divider. So he cut back to the right, causing our vehicle to fishtail. That's when the pickup hit us.

"I never even saw you," the driver told us.

Fortunately, no one was injured, and we were able, after giving our statements to the police, to continue our journey home. The red truck was totaled. Although two motorists stopped to make sure no one was injured, neither stayed to give statements to the police. The investigating officer determined the other driver was at fault. His insurance company paid for the repairs to our vehicle, as well as for a rental car while the repairs were being made.

End of story? No.

Three months later the insurance company called and told us a witness had come forth and said that we were at fault, that we cut in front of the pickup and caused the collision. When I paid a visit to my insurance company, I read an amended report that put us at fault, yet we never received a copy of that report. Neither did we receive any further communication from the South Carolina State Highway Patrol. No citation. No fine. Nothing. I called the investigating officer three times to find out what was going on, but my call was never returned.

So where, after three months, did this witness come from? And why, after that long, did he come forward, when there were no injuries and the damage was relatively minor? I knew we were telling the truth. I had my doubts about this new witness. But how do you defend yourself against a lie?

By telling the truth and waiting for it to prevail.

And by praying. During my quiet time, God spoke to me through His Word:

"A lying witness is unconvincing; a person who speaks the truth is respected" (Proverbs 21:28 The Message).

"Unscrupulous people fake it a lot, honest people are sure of their steps" (v. 29).

"Nothing clever, nothing conceived, nothing contrived, can get the better of God" (v. 30).

"Do your best, prepare for the worst, then trust God to bring the victory" (v. 31).

After giving our statements again, this time to our insurance company, we heard nothing more about it until December when the other driver called our home.

"This has been dragging on too long," he said, adding that our insurance company had determined not to accept this witness's testimony.

When King David fled Jerusalem because his son Absalom rebelled and seized the throne, a servant by the name of Ziba lied about his master, Mephibosheth, the crippled son of David's dear friend Jonathan. Ziba told David that Mephibosheth stayed in Jerusalem to support Absalom. That was a lie so he could get in the king's good graces and acquire Mephibosheth's property. The truth eventually came out, and Ziba's treachery was exposed.

"Sin has many tools," wrote Oliver Wendell Holmes, "but a lie is the handle that fits them all."

I still feel helpless against a lie. But I've learned that lies may travel faster, but truth sticks around longer.

"Therefore put on the full armor of God, so that when the day of evil comes, you may be able to stand your ground, and after you have done everything, to stand. Stand firm then, with the belt of truth buckled around your waist" (Ephesians 6:13-14 NIV).

When I feel threatened and helpless in the face of a lie, remind me, Lord, that truth will eventually win out. Amen.

MORE TEA:

Read and reflect on 2 Samuel 16:1–4, 19:24–30; Psalm 119:129–144.

The Better Bone

You shall not covet. –Exodus 20:17 NIV

A heart at peace gives life to the body, but envy rots the bones. –Proverbs 14:30 NIV

ONE MORNING I GAVE each of our dogs, Bobby and Charlie, a big, juicy venison bone before I sat down for my devotions.

That'll keep them quiet and occupied for awhile, I thought smugly as they settled on the living room carpet about six feet from each other.

I sank down onto the love seat and opened my Bible to the day's meditation. After a few minutes, Bobby got up, dropped his bone on the carpet at my feet, and stood over Charlie until she let go of hers. Quickly, he snapped it up and scooted behind the love seat. Charlie was too surprised to growl.

I didn't want a dogfight in the middle of my living room, so I picked up Bobby's bone and gave it to Charlie. It wasn't long before Bobby sneaked out from behind the love seat and, once again, snatched the bone Charlie was chomping on. I took the bone that Bobby had left and dropped it in front of Charlie. Catching on to Bobby's thievery, Charlie left the bone I gave her and went after Bobby's.

On and on the swapping went, each dog acting as though the other had the better bone. What I thought would make for peace, instead became a source of envy and caused trouble.

I, too, battle envy. When a friend drives by in a new vehicle, suddenly my eight-year-old Explorer looks rustier and rattles more loudly. After I've visited with someone who has a nicer house than I have, it seems as though the furniture and carpeting in my house have gotten shabbier overnight. And it's all too easy to find fault with those who I feel are smarter, thinner, or more talented.

Nine of the Ten Commandments deal with our actions; the tenth deals with our inner desires: "You must not be envious of your neighbor's house, or want to sleep with his wife, or want to own his slaves, oxen, donkeys, or anything else he has" (Exodus 20:17 LB).

Like an acid, envy eats away at my peace of mind, my inner joy and contentment, and my relationships with others. No wonder God tells us to rid ourselves of envy (1 Peter 2:1). He knows what I'm still learning—that love, not envy, is the better bone.

When I feel that tug of envy on my heart, O Lord, help me to be satisfied with what I have, for everything I have is a gift from You. Amen.

MORE TEA:

Read and reflect on Matthew 6:19–33; Psalm 119:145–160.

For further study: Hebrews 13:5; Philippians 4:11–13; James 1:17; Psalm 145:14–21; 1Timothy 6:9–11; Colossians 3:5; Matthew 15:19–20.

The Greatest Commandment

For the LORD does not see as man sees; for man looks at the outward appearance, but the LORD looks at the heart. –1 Samuel 16:7 NKJV

ACCORDING TO THE MERCK Manual, an online source of medical information, vascular disease is a leading cause of death in the Western world. Arteriosclerosis, commonly known as hardening of the arteries, is a silent killer, as gradually the walls of the arteries, which carry the blood to vital body organs such as the brain and the heart, become hardened and thick with plaque, restricting the flow of blood. When blood can't get to the brain, a person suffers a stroke. When it can't get to the heart, a heart attack occurs.

Most of the time, a person doesn't know his arteries are becoming blocked until physical symptoms, such as chest pain, occurs. Often there is no warning. A person may appear healthy and strong until suddenly a heart attack or stroke takes his or her life.

Life is in the blood (Leviticus 17:14), and what pumps this life-giving liquid throughout the body? The heart. But our hearts are only as healthy as our blood vessels.

Over the past several pages, we've delved into the Ten Commandments, exploring how these 3,450-year-old laws apply to us today. But which of the ten is the most important?

One of the rulers during Jesus' day asked Him the same question.

Jesus' answer? "Love the Lord your God with all your heart and with all your soul and with all your mind and with all your strength" (Mark 12:30 NIV). Heart, soul, mind, and strength represent the total person: emotional, spiritual, mental, and physical.

But is that possible? Can we finite human beings love anyone or anything so completely?

I know I struggle with loving God the way He demands to be loved. Too much of myself gets in the way. Like the rich young man who came to Jesus and asked, "What must I do to be saved?" (Mark 10:17–30), I, too, struggle with "one thing you lack." There always seems to be something that gets in the way of total surrender. It might be feelings and attitudes of envy, self-pity, smoldering anger or resentment, or perhaps it's a bad habit I refuse to give up or wanting my own way rather than God's way.

These unhealthy feelings and attitudes, also known as sin, are the plaque that builds up in my spiritual blood vessels, restricting the flow of life-giving blood to my heart. Sin is the leading—and only—cause of spiritual death.

According to the Bible, our hearts have been giving us trouble since the beginning.

"The heart is deceitful above all things and beyond cure," the prophet Jeremiah wrote, "Who can understand it?" (Jeremiah 17:9 NIV)

"These people come near to me with their mouth and honor me with their lips, but their hearts are far from me," God said through the prophet Isaiah (Isaiah 29:13 NIV).

So, what is the cure for our sin-plagued, hardened hearts?

"Rid yourselves of all the offenses you have committed," God commands in Ezekiel 18:31, "and get a new heart and a new spirit."

But how? We are powerless to cleanse and purify our own hearts. We must turn to the Great Physician, the Healer of our hearts.

"Create in me a clean heart, O God," David wrote in Psalm 51:10, "and renew a right spirit within me."

"If we confess our sins, He is faithful and just to forgive us our sins and to cleanse us from all unrighteousness," the apostle John wrote (1 John 1:9 NKJV).

"I will give them an undivided heart and put a new spirit in them," God promises through Ezekiel (11:19 NIV). "I will remove from them their heart of stone and give them a heart of flesh."

Only when my heart has been softened, cleansed, and renewed by the hand of God; only when the sin-plaque is carved out of my stubborn will; only when my heart has been changed can I truly love Him as He demands to be loved. Then and only then, with a changed heart, will I find the Ten Commandments— all ten of them—easy to obey.

Create in me a clean heart, O God, and renew a right spirit within me (Psalm 51:10 ESV). Amen.

MORE TEA:

Read and reflect on Mark 12:28–34; Psalm 119:161–176.

Tests of Faith

Count it all joy ...
when you meet various trials,
for you know that the testing of your faith
produces steadfastness.

–James 1:2–3 RSV

Cast or Carry?

Cast your burden on the LORD, and he will sustain you. – Psalm 55:22 ESV

I RECENTLY READ ABOUT a twenty-five-year-old Army veteran suffering from degenerative arthritis.

"Arthritis is supposed to happen when you get old," he told a *Seattle Times* reporter. "What's it going to be like when I'm fifty or sixty?"

The arthritis caused painful bone spurs in the vertebrae in his neck and can be traced to carrying seventy to eighty pounds of equipment when he served in Iraq. The human body is just not made to lift and carry heavy loads. Even with training, you can only carry so much.

Likewise, the human spirit can only carry so much for so long.

Burdens. Physical, mental, emotional, spiritual. We all have to deal with them. They come with living in this world.

How do we deal with burdens?

According to my Bible, we either carry them or cast them.

Take Moses, for example. He carried the burden of leading the contrary, complaining people of Israel from Egypt to the Promised Land.

"You lay the burden of all these people on me," he said to God at one point.

So God told him to select seventy men from the elders. "I will take some of the Spirit that is on you and put it on them, and they shall bear the burden of the people with you, so that you may not bear it yourself alone" (Numbers 11:17 ESV).

We are not meant to bear our burdens alone.

"Bear one another's burdens," God's Word instructs us, "and so fulfill the law of Christ" (Galatians 6:2 NKJV).

Isn't it so much easier when even one person comes alongside us and helps us? The thing about helping others is that when we get our minds off our own burdens and help someone else with theirs, ours don't seem to be as heavy.

And then there's Jesus. "Come to me," He says, "all of you who are weary and carry heavy burdens, and I will give you rest" (Matthew 11:28 NLT).

How do we give Jesus our burdens to carry?

We cast them on Him.

"Cast your burden on the LORD," David tells us, "and he will sustain you" (Psalm 55:22 ESV).

And if anyone had burdens to bear, it was him. Anointed king over Israel, David spent years in the wilderness, hiding in caves, fleeing from the murderous King Saul. And when he did become king, his own son attempted to usurp the throne. Yet read the psalms of David, and you'll see he learned to cast his burdens on the Lord.

Peter tells us to "cast all your anxieties (cares, worries) on him because he cares for you" (1 Peter 5:7 ESV).

How do you cast your worries on God, give your burden to Jesus to carry?

First, refuse to allow your mind to dwell on your anxieties. Acknowledge them, don't deny them, and release them through prayer (see Philippians 4:6–7). Imagine them soaring up to heaven, where God will take care of them, in His way and in His time.

Replace your worried thoughts with thoughts that are true, noble, right, pure, lovely, admirable, excellent, praiseworthy (Philippians 4:8).

Celebrate the good things in your life. Keep a gratitude journal and write in it every day. And rejoice!

I'm still working on learning how to cast my cares on God, completely.

What burdens do you need to release to Him?

Help me, Lord, to cast all my care on You every moment of every day. Show me someone who needs help carrying their burden. Amen.

MORE TEA: Read and reflect on Matthew 11:28–29.

Turning a Setback into a Comeback

No, dear brothers and sisters, I have not achieved it, but I focus on this one thing: Forgetting the past and looking forward to what lies ahead. – Philippians 3:13 NLT

A YEAR AGO I was a mess physically. Overweight, tired all the time, pushing through each day joylessly, miserable when I got on the scale and even more so when I looked in the mirror, and wrestling with insomnia night after night, despite sleeping pills.

I knew the answer lay in what I ate. I'd tried just about every diet out there, and mostly they worked—for a while. I'd lose a few pounds, start feeling good, then revert to my default mode. After all, how could a Slovak gal like me resist pasta and bread?

But a year ago I came to the end of my rope. I needed help. So I contacted a certified nutritional therapy practitioner. And my life changed.

Amy Taladay taught me a lot not just about the right foods, but about my own body and its response to the foods I eat. Within a month foggy-headedness disappeared, energy returned, pounds dropped off, and for the first time in years, I was able to sleep without sleeping pills. Folks told me my skin glowed.

Finally! Not a diet, but an eating plan I could live with for the rest of my life.

Then I went on vacation. A granola bar here, a slice of pizza there, and soon I was in default mode. Not entirely, but, hey, I wasn't reacting to the food, so maybe I was healed of whatever it was that caused all my issues.

Oh, what a tangled web we weave when first we practice to deceive! And that includes deceiving ourselves. By March, the gluten rash returned with a vengeance, as did the insomnia, fatigue, and brain fog. The numbers on my scale inched up.

Back to square one. But at least I knew where square one was, and at least I have the resources to get back on track with what I call my vibrant health plan.

I will turn this setback into a comeback.

Peter, too, failed miserably, doing the very thing he boasted he'd never do—deny Jesus. "And he left the courtyard, weeping bitterly" (Luke 22:62 NLT). Yet less than two months later, we see Peter preaching boldly to a crowd of thousands in the very city where he denied Jesus (Acts 2:14–41). Of that crowd, three thousand became believers.

Now, that's turning a setback into a comeback!

How do you turn your setback into a comeback?

First, stop denying and face the truth about yourself. For me, it was accepting the fact that certain foods cause distress to my body and I need to avoid them—for the rest of my life.

Second, truly repent, which means "to feel or express sincere regret or remorse about one's wrongdoing." The negative effects of the foods I shouldn't have eaten caused me great regret and remorse.

Third, determine not to make that mistake again and commit to a positive, corrective course of action. For me, I committed to following my vibrant health plan to the letter, even though it takes hours in planning and preparation. The time spent is worth it.

Fourth, seek the counsel of those wiser and more knowledgeable and the support of those who truly care about you. I'm blessed to have a husband who encourages me to eat the right foods and is willing to eat whatever I make, whether it's a flop or a hit. And to have the support of my prayer team, precious friends who uphold my writing and speaking ministry. They know whatever affects my body will affect my ministry.

Fifth, pray, asking for wisdom, guidance, and supernatural enabling. "For I can do everything through Christ, who gives me strength" (Philippians 4:13 NLT).

And finally, let go of past mistakes. Learn from them and move on. Pursue the vision of whatever goal God has placed in your heart.

Lord, give me the strength, wisdom, and courage to turn this setback into a comeback. And I will give You the honor and the glory. Amen.

MORE TEA: Read and reflect on Luke 22:31–34, 54–62.

When Faith Fails

"Did I not say to you that if you would believe you would see the glory of God?" –Jesus, as quoted in John 11:44 NKJV

WHEN HER HUSBAND, JIM, was speared to death by the Auca Indians he was trying to reach with the Gospel, Elisabeth Elliot, who'd just turned twenty-nine a month earlier, was left with a ten-month-old daughter.

Yet Elisabeth didn't pull up stakes and return to the US. She remained in Ecuador, living among and ministering to the Quichua tribe, continuing the work she and Jim began. She chose believe God, His Word, and His promises, despite the circumstances. In time, she served as a missionary to the very tribe that killed her husband.

While scant few believers will ever experience a trial by fire like Elisabeth did, we all eventually come to a point where we feel faith has failed us.

When are those times?

When others fail you. You've been betrayed, lied to, used by someone you trusted. Or perhaps someone made a promise, sincere at the time, they didn't fulfill. More than once.

What then?

Check on *where* your faith resides.

Remember King David. He was betrayed over and over throughout his life—by close friends, by his own son. He chose not to become bitter, but to forgive and move on. That didn't mean he trusted those who failed him. It means he chose to acknowledge we humans are an imperfect lot. I know I've failed others many times. I'm thankful for grace, mercy, forgiveness, and second chances.

David knew where he could put his faith and it wouldn't fail him: "It is better to trust in the LORD than to put confidence in man" (Psalm 118:8 NKJV). God will never let you down.

Another time your faith falters is *when you don't get what you ask for in prayer*. Your requests to the Almighty aren't answered when and how you think they should. Or you think they haven't been answered at all.

What then?

Ask yourself: Is my faith in prayer or in the One who hears and answers? God will never let you down. Your loving Father knows what is best for you. His answers are always exactly what and when you need them.

Remember Psalm 5:3: "In the morning, Lord, you hear my voice; in the morning I lay my requests before you and wait expectantly."

Another time faith may fail is *when you don't get the promised rewards for your obedience*. You've given your time, talent, and treasure to God, to the church, to worthy causes, often at great sacrifice, expecting the windows of heaven to open and a blessing so great, you don't have room enough to receive it (Malachi 3:10).

Yet the windows remain firmly shut and your coffers empty.

What then?

Check your motives. Are you obeying out of love for God or for the rewards you want?

Maybe you've received your rewards, but you just can't see them. Look again. This time with eyes opened by divine perspective.

Who says all our rewards are monetary, material? What about good health? What about receiving just what you need when you need it? What about the respect of others? A good reputation? The love of your spouse and children? A roof over your head? Food on the table? Enough money in the bank to pay the bills (sometimes just enough)? A cup of tea (or coffee) with a friend? Eyes to see the sky in all its moods, the sun as it rises and sets, the birds at the birdfeeder? Ears to hear the wind in the trees, the gurgling of a brook, the roar of the ocean …

Blessings are all around us, if only we have the eyes of faith to see them.

Remember: "My God shall supply *all* your need *according to His riches* in glory" (Philippians 4:19 NKJV, emphasis mine).

Others will fail you, prayers won't get answered when and how you want them to, and you won't always get what you think you deserve.

But our faithful God will never leave you or forsake you (Hebrews 13:5). And that's a promise you can count on.

Lord, I believe! Help my unbelief. Increase my faith. Amen.

MORE TEA: Read and reflect on John 11:1–44.

The Certainty of Uncertainty

How do you know what is going to happen tomorrow? For the length of your lives is as uncertain as the morning fog—now you see it; soon it is gone. –James 4:14 TLB

LIFE CAN TURN ON a dime.

A thirty-nine-year-old wife and mother is diagnosed with ALS—progressive, incurable. One minute she's raising her kids, planning for the future, and the next all those hopes and dreams come crashing down around her. How to tell her three children?

A ninety-seven-year-old woman losing her eyesight waits in a personal care home, longing for the day God calls her home. But before that happens, she learns she has cancer.

A fifty-seven-year-old husband, father, and grandfather is sent home to hospice care, which barely lasts a week, leaving his family devastated and his young grandchildren dealing with a grief they cannot understand.

A fifty-nine-year-old doting grandmother faces months, even years, of recovery after a head-on collision, which the other driver caused. Not to mention the insurance hassles.

A young man, twenty-four, his divorced mother's only child, loses his fight with drug addiction.

Divorce. Unemployment. Suicide. The list goes on.

When these things happen, you realize you'd rather deal with the question marks of life than the certainty of the long, dark valley stretching ahead of you. The valley of progressive, incurable disease. The valley of waiting. The valley of grief. But you have no choice. It is what it is.

How do you cope with the certainty of life's uncertainty?

By focusing on five things that *are* certain (besides death, taxes, and uncertainty):

God's love: unlimited, unchanging, steadfast, and eternal (Psalm 36:5). It's yours for the taking.

"For I am convinced," wrote the apostle Paul, whose life was as uncertain as a ship tossed on stormy seas, "that neither death nor life, neither angels nor demons, neither the present nor the future, nor any powers, neither height nor depth, nor anything else in all creation, will be able to separate us from the love of God that is in Christ Jesus our Lord" (Romans 8:37–39 NIV).

God's presence. "Yea, though I walk through the valley of the shadow of death, I will fear no evil; for You are with me; Your rod and Your staff, they comfort me" (Psalm 23:4 NKJV). (See also Hebrews 13:5.)

God's provision. "Look at the birds of the air," says Jesus, "they do not sow, nor reap nor gather into barns, and yet your heavenly Father feeds them. Are you not worth much more than they?" (Matthew 6:26). He not only provides food, He also gives you rest (Psalm 23, Matthew 11:28), peace (John 14:27), and wisdom (James 1:5).

God's sustaining grace. God didn't remove Paul's "thorn in the flesh," instead He told the apostle His grace was all he needed. God may not remove your burden, but He will give His grace to sustain you through the valley.

Your *future.* No, not your future on earth, but your home in heaven. "For we know that when this earthly tent we live in is taken down (that is, when we die and leave this earthly body), we will have a house in heaven, an eternal body made for us by God himself and not by human hands" (2 Corinthians 5:1 AMP).

The mother-in-law of the woman diagnosed with ALS told her son to stress to the children not to allow fear of the future to rob them of joy with their mother today.

"In all these things," writes the apostle Paul, "we are more than conquerors through Him who loved us" (Romans 8:37 NKJV).

Yes, life can change in a heartbeat. But God—His steadfast love, amazing grace, abiding presence, abundant provision—will never change.

Of that you can be certain.

What uncertainties are you facing?

Help me, O God, to keep my eyes fixed on You, not on the long, dark valley stretching before me. Remind me You will never leave me, never abandon me, never forsake me. That You are right here with me. Help me not to let fear rob me of joy, no matter what the circumstances. Amen.

MORE TEA: Read and reflect on 2 Corinthians 4:7–5:5.

When Storms Assail

You will keep him in perfect peace, whose mind is stayed on You, because he trusts in You. –Isaiah 26:3 NKJV

AS I WROTE THIS meditation, Hurricane Florence was churning her way ashore, her eye on the Carolinas. My daughter, Jaime, lives in South Carolina, so my mother's eye watched the track of that monstrous storm. Torrential rains and tropical-storm-force winds were forecast to extend far inland.

"Come home," I suggested to her.

"I couldn't even if I wanted to," she said. "Over a million folks evacuating the coast are on the highways heading west.

So Jaime prepared the best she could, hunkered down, and rode it out.

Storms assail no matter where we live, whether they be hurricanes, tornadoes, earthquakes, floods, mudslides, rainstorms, snowstorms, windstorms, or another natural disaster. At any place in the world, at any given time, disaster can strike. That doesn't mean we live in fear or let worry consume us.

It means we do all we can to prepare, then hunker down and ride it out—and leave the outcome in God's hands.

This goes for storms not of a physical nature, too—those emotional, mental, spiritual tempests. They can be circumstances, relationships, situations. Whatever the cause, they impact us profoundly and shatter our illusions of a smooth, easy sail through life.

Some storms, like hurricanes, we know are coming, so we can prepare. Some, like tornadoes or earthquakes, catch us unaware. But unaware doesn't mean unprepared.

How can we prepare for the storms of life that are sure to come?

First, know they *will* come. No one is immune from the trials and tribulations that assail our existence on this planet. Even Jesus assured us, "In the world you will have trouble" (John 16:33). In the same statement, He gave us a way to cope: "I have told you these things, so that in me you may have peace." Are you *in Him*?

Second, stock up on the essentials. Just like the folks preparing for the storm stock up on food and water, so, too, stock up on the Bread of Life and the Living Water (John 6:35 and John 4:10, 14) to keep your spirit strong. Do this by filling your mind and heart with His Word. Like the bread and water you consume physically is broken down and its nutrients absorbed by the body, so the words of The Word are absorbed into your mind and heart to nourish your spirit.

Third, make sure you have an alternate source of power. In a physical storm, the chances of losing power increase in proportion with the strength of the storm. So fresh batteries are on the stock-up list. So, too, with your spiritual storms. You know where the Source of Power is—God—and that Power will never go out. All you have to do is plug into it through prayer. Ask for strength, courage, wisdom, and whatever else you need to weather the storm.

Jesus told us to ask and we *will* receive (Matthew 7:7). That's why it's important to consume the Word so that it will abide in you and you can draw on its strength and power when you need it.

Fourth, just like folks prepare for the storm by barricading their windows, so, too, barricade your spirit with the protection only God can give. He Himself is a shield around you (Psalm 3:3). His are the wings under which you find refuge (Psalm 91:4). His angels have charge over you (Psalm 91:11).

Finally, hunker down with trust. Trust that, like Jesus knew His disciples were fighting the wind and the waves, God knows the tempest you're facing. And like Jesus came to His disciples in the midst of the storm, so He will come to you. Indeed, He never left you (Hebrews 13:5, Matthew 28:20).

Let His command to the wind and the waves, "Peace! Be still!" reverberate in your mind and heart, and settle in your spirit.

Facing a storm? Prepare the best you can, hunker down, then ride it out, remembering God Himself is with you in the midst of your storm.

When storms assail, remind me, dear Lord, that You are all I need to survive them. Amen.

MORE TEA:

Read and reflect on Mark 4:35–41; Mark 6:45–51; Psalm 91.

Forging a New Normal

Do all things without complaining or grumbling or questioning the providence of God. –Philippians 2:14

IT WASN'T WHAT I wanted to hear.

After months of nearly constant lower back pain that increasingly worsened, trips to two doctors (my PCP and my orthopaedic doctor), X-rays, and a CT scan, I made an appointment with the spine surgeon who'd operated on my neck eight years earlier. That surgery went well, and I was able to resume my normal life after recovery. I'd hoped the same would be true this time.

"I want to walk and hike again without pain," I told the nurse who compiled my information. As well as sleep without the constant ache that invaded my slumber and woke me up through the night.

"I can't promise you that," she said.

Surgery wasn't an option. Operating on the lower back, as opposed to operating on the neck, is a totally different ballgame.

There is no cure for my diagnosis: degenerative arthritis, also called osteoarthritis. Add to the mix herniated disks, bone spurs, and scoliosis (a slight curving of the spine in same area as the arthritis). The scoliosis, I was told, is probably why I have pain, stiffness, and a feeling of instability when I wake up or when I work at the kitchen counter. The back brace I bought helps some.

Instead of surgery, what the doctor prescribed was physical therapy, cortisone shots, and various medications. No quick fix.

No fix at all, as far as I was concerned. I'd rather pursue natural remedies when it comes to health issues. I wanted to avoid the injections. Research into the prescribed medicines revealed two of the three would interact with my blood pressure medicine.

What it boils down is a lifestyle change. Just what I want as I approach the seventh decade of life.

Of course I had my grumbling, complaining, and pouting sessions. I've been grumbling and complaining for months. My poor little flock (I'm the lay pastor for a small church in Punxsutawney)—graciously listened to me gripe every week. And DH—the word *longsuffering* was coined for this man.

What now?

Time to put on my big girl britches and deal with it. Learn to live with it. Without kvetching. Forge a new normal. Alter my horizons, change my goals, adjust the pace at which I tackle my day. Shorten that to-do list and incorporate physical therapy, exercise, walking, stretches, rest, and meal planning. Educate myself through research.

In addition to pursuing my dream of writing. Sitting for long periods of time is a no-no, but unfortunately that's par for the writer's course. So I bought a Fitbit, which reminds me to get up and walk every hour. Not that I always heed it.

It never ceases to amaze me how God meets us in our deepest valleys.

During my quiet time, I've been reading *Draw the Circle: The 40-Day Prayer Challenge* by Mark Batterson. Not following the day-by-day readings, but choosing the selections randomly.

As I wrestled with the diagnosis and the resulting life changes this past week, God led me to Day 4: "Don't Pray Away." Batterson related the story of a couple whose three-year-old son fell from a second-story window and was permanently paralyzed.

Here's what John Tiller, the father, wrote: "It was time to accept his current condition and choose to live life with disability.... Instead of getting discouraged or getting angry, I choose to look for what God can do."

"Sometimes," wrote Batterson, "the purpose of prayer is to get *out of* circumstances, but more often than not, the purpose of prayer is to *get us through* them."

There was nothing random about choosing this selection on that particular day, a day when I needed those words the most.

What a God!

Sustain me with Your grace, help me to stand firm in Your strength, and give me the determination to keep putting one step in front of the other. Amen.

MORE TEA: Read and reflect on 2 Corinthians 12:7–10.

Trio of Trouble

Oh, give thanks to the LORD for He is good! For His mercy endures forever. – Psalm 107:1 NKJV

I GOT UP EARLY one Sunday morning to work on my sermon, but the bottom two rows of my computer keyboard didn't work. I couldn't even use the spacebar.

Then, on the way to church, we had a flat tire on the camper. We'd planned to leave for the Allegheny National Forest for a camping trip right after church.

On Monday morning, I put in my hearing aids, but one didn't work. After I changed the battery, it still didn't work.

"It's dead," I told DH. "Kaput."

I couldn't get an appointment with my hearing aid guy for two weeks. So for two weeks I felt off-balance and out of sync. And for two weeks asked "What?" a lot.

I lamented on Facebook, listing my trio of woes.

"Trouble comes in threes," one friend commented. "I'm so happy *all* your troubles are over!"

If only.

"God is good," people say when their prayers are answered in the manner they want. When unexpected blessings come their way. When life is smooth sailing.

But how many say "God is good" when their prayers *aren't* answered the way they want, and heaven's blessing doors seem shut tight? Do they say "God is good" when trouble comes and moves in for an extended stay?

We sing, "God is good *all the time*," but do we live the lyrics?

We should. Because the God we believe in on the mountain is still God in the valleys of our lives. "The God of the good times is still God in the bad times. The God of the day is still God in the night."*

I'm learning firsthand the truth of the words Paul wrote to the Philippian believers: "Don't worry about anything; instead, pray about everything. Tell God what you need, and thank him for all he has done. Then you will experience God's peace, which exceeds anything we can understand. His peace will guard your hearts and minds as you live in Christ Jesus" (Philippians 4:6–7 NLT).

Over and over these words have come to mind this year. This Scripture has become my theme verse for the year—not one I chose at the beginning of January, but one that chose me through life experiences.

And so I've refused to fret over the broken keyboard, the flat tire, and the dead hearing aid. Although money is tight with DH being retired now.

I ordered a new keyboard, which I'm still getting used to. (I miss my old one.) At a little over thirty dollars, it didn't break the bank.

We went camping on the spare tire. And had one of the most wonderfully relaxing, refreshing, and rejuvenating trips in a long time.

DH determined we needed to replace all four tires on the camper, since they were on when it bought it last year and we didn't know how many miles they'd traveled. Gulp! But he did his research, and the final bill totaled a couple hundred less than what we first figured. (Is anyone out there in the market for some good but used camper tires?) And it just so happened we received an unexpected refund in the mail for a medical bill we'd paid.

And finally, the dead hearing aid. When I visited my hearing aid guy, he discovered the problem wasn't in the aid itself but in a replaceable filter. Instead of over a grand or more for a new hearing aid, I paid the usual twenty-five dollars for a clean and check.

"God has a reason for allowing things to happen," I read online. "We may never understand His wisdom, but we simply have to trust His will."

All in all, it could have been worse. I am blessed. God is good. Even when trouble comes in threes.

Those who are wise will take all this to heart; they will see in our history the faithful love of the LORD. –Psalm 107:43 NLT

Remind me, Lord, when troubles come, that You are still in control and I am still blessed. Amen.

MORE TEA: Read and reflect on Psalm 37.

The Risk of Prayer

So I say to you: Ask and it will be given to you; seek and you will find; knock and the door will be opened to you. For everyone who asks receives; the one who seeks finds; and to the one who knocks, the door will be opened. –Jesus, as quoted in Luke 11:9–10 NIV

IN HIS BOOK, *Draw the Circle: The 40 Day Prayer Challenge*, Mark Batterson tells about an African missionary whose church met beneath the shade of a tree near the village because they didn't have a building in which to worship. The local witch doctor wasn't too happy with that, so he cursed the tree and it withered.

When you preach Christ and His power, when you preach an awesome God who can do the impossible, when you preach the powerful presence of the indwelling Spirit, you better be ready to stand firm. Trials always come to test your faith, especially when you proclaim it.

In response, the missionary called for a public prayer meeting during which he laid hands on the tree and asked God to resurrect it.

In public. Where everyone could hear him.

"If God doesn't answer his prayer," Batterson wrote, "he would have dug an even deeper hole. That's the risk of prayer, isn't it?"

That made me think. How often do we say "safe" prayers, all in the realm of the possible? Do we have the courage to pray the impossible prayers? Or do we pray them, but give ourselves an out?

"Sometimes," Batterson noted, "God calls us to ante up all the faith we have, and then let the chips fall where they may."

When I read this devotional, appropriately titled "Shameless Audacity," DH and I were in a real pickle. Two days earlier the transmission went in our pickup while towing the camper to a campground. Now, while we sat at the campground, the truck sat in the towing company's lot, waiting for us to decide what to do with it.

Rebuilding the transmission would cost anywhere from $3,800 to $4,600. With taxes coming due in another month, the fuel oil tank needing replenished before winter, DH retired for nearly a year, and us living on a very limited income, where would the money come from? The extended warranty (that's another story) expired in April.

It just so happened (translate: God-thing) a Christian couple were camped a few sites up from us. On one of his walks around the campground, DH stopped and talked to them. They, as well as everyone in the campground, knew of our predicament. After all, a tow truck had backed our camper in our site then left with our truck.

So they prayed with DH—that the truck would be fixed at no cost to us! Now that's a bold prayer!

Bold prayers take bold faith. Shameless audacity.

Shameless means disregard for that others may say or think. Audacity is a willingness to take bold risks.

Faith calls us to believe nothing is impossible with God. "It's the impossible prayers that honor God because they reveal our faith and allow God to reveal His glory," Batterson noted.

I thought about the impossible scenarios in the Bible: the Red Sea parting and the Israelites walking across on dry ground. The walls of Jericho falling down flat without a hand touching them. Barren Sarah and one-hundred-year-old Abraham having a baby. The virgin birth of Jesus. His miracles. His resurrection.

God specializes in the impossible!

If God can speak the universe into being, can He not take our impossible situations and turn them into HIM-possible ones?

Jesus said to ask, seek, and knock. He promises that what we ask will be provided, what we seek we'll find, and the door will open when we knock.

Oh, yes, the withered tree … "Not only did God break the curse and resurrect the tree," Batterson wrote, "it became the only tree of its type to yield its fruit not once, but twice a year. A double crop! A double blessing!"

What impossible situation are you faced with today? What bold prayer do you need to pray?

Remember, sometimes you've got to ante up all the faith you have, pray with shameless audacity, and let the chips fall where they may.

Dear God, give me the holy boldness to pray the impossible prayers. Amen.

MORE TEA: Read and reflect on Luke 11:5–9; 18:1–8; James 1:2–4.

The Birds of the Air

"Give your entire attention to what God is doing right now, and don't get worked up about what may or may not happen tomorrow. God will help you deal with whatever hard things come up when the time comes."–Jesus, as quoted in Matthew 6:34 The Message

IT WAS LITERALLY THE birds of the air that caught my attention one morning during my quiet time.

The morning temperatures were still warm enough to sit out on the back deck and absorb the peacefulness of the woods behind my house. I'd not slept well the night before, my mind whirring with worries.

I know—Christians aren't supposed to worry, right? But life slams Christians, too. What makes it different for us is how we respond to it.

And I wasn't responding very well. Not as well as I thought I would. It's easy to spout Scripture when things are going relatively smoothly. But when the storms come, the winds tear at your faith, and the waves crash over your resolve to stand firm, it's all you can do to hang on.

Scripture tells us to cast all our cares on Him because He cares for us (1 Peter 5:7) and He'll sustain us (Psalm 55:22). It's one thing to read those words; it's another story entirely to do them.

Now, I'm good at casting. The problem is I keep reeling the burden back in. And casting it out again. And reeling it back in.

That night I cast my burden on the Lord by presenting Him with the whole list of what was worrying me. I claimed Philippians 4:19—that God will supply all that I needed. And, in keeping with Luke 11:9, I asked. I sought. I knocked.

Now if only I could leave the response to Him.

But no. I awoke the next morning with the burden still heavy on my mind, heart, and spirit.

The little gray bird flitting from limb to limb caught my eye first. Then the robin, worm still in its beak.

"Look at the birds of the air," I heard God say. "They neither sow nor reap nor gather into barns, and yet your heavenly Father feeds them. Are you not of more value than they?" (Matthew 6:26 ESV)

I looked up the Scripture—Matthew 6:25–34. Three times Jesus said, "Do not worry."

And I remembered Philippians 4:6—"Don't be anxious or worried about anything."

I did the second part of that verse—"pray about everything. Tell God what you need, and thank him for all he has done." But peace still eluded me. Because I kept reeling those worries back in again and again.

"Worry is like a rocking chair," motivational speaker Glenn Turner noted. "It gives you something to do but it gets you nowhere."

I'm not good at sitting still and waiting for God to work. I have to be doing something—anything but be still.

"I have come, that they might have life," Jesus said, "life in all its fullness" (John 10:10). Abundant life.

And worry compromises that abundant life by siphoning your hope, your joy, your energy, and replacing them with anxiety, insomnia, tension, and irritability. In other words, you're no fun to live with.

So, how do we deal with worry?

First, recognize where it comes from: the enemy of our souls, a lack of trust in God, and a weak faith. That's a hard pill to swallow.

Second, respond to it by praying: cast your burdens on the Lord and *leave them there*! Prioritize that worry list. Determine what's most important and, with prayer, deal with that.

And finally, live in the present.

"Worry is carrying tomorrow's load with today's strength—carrying two days at once," said holocaust survivor Corrie ten Boom. "It is moving into tomorrow ahead of time. Worry does not empty tomorrow of its troubles. It empties today of its strength."

Look at your calendar. See that square marked *today?* Focus on that. Live in one square at a time.

Do you dwell on the what if's—what if this? What if that?

Do you focus on the worst-case scenario?

Do you lie awake at night because your worries are whirring through your mind and you just can't put them to bed?

Maybe, like me, you need more practice with your casting—and learning not to reel them back in.

When I thought, "My foot slips," your steadfast love, O LORD, held me up. When the cares of my heart are many, your consolations cheer my soul. –Psalm 94:18–19 ESV

MORE TEA: Read and reflect on Matthew 6:25–34.

TO THE READER

I titled my very first book of meditations, published in 2000, *Minute Meditations: Meeting God in Everyday Experiences.* That's the bottom line, the core message, of my writing and speaking ministries: the abiding presence of God.

It is my prayer that, as you read the meditations in this book, you too became aware of His presence in your life. You saw the many ways He's walked beside you, helped you through the tough times, assured you He'd never leave you or forsake you. During the times He was silent and you wondered why, you clung to the promises in His Word.

As you look back at your life journey, you see how faithful He has been to you. You understand the difference between religion and relationship. Religion, as Christian author Fritz Ridenour explains in his book *How to be a Christian Without Being Religious*, is man's efforts to reach up to God. Which will never work. (Read Isaiah 6:1–6.) God is too holy for sinful us to ever come near.

However, God provided a way for that sin to be removed so we can have a relationship with Him. Since only a perfect sacrifice would remove sin, and there's no way we'll ever be perfect, God reached down to us in the Person of His Son, Jesus. This Perfect One went to the cross to take the punishment for our sins so that we are forgiven, washed clean, rid of that sin stain and guilt once and for all.

Maybe you know all this and have a relationship with Him through His Son, Jesus. You know beyond a shadow of a doubt where you'll be when your life journey here on earth ends (1 John 5:11–12).

But perhaps you don't. Perhaps you've never really heard the Gospel—the Good News that you can be forgiven and free. Perhaps you've heard the Good News but put it on the back burner for a better time. There were too many things you wanted to do before you "got religion."

But God's never stopped pursuing you. Perhaps you sense He's calling you, drawing you to Him, inviting you to a higher and deeper relationship with Him. You hear Him, in someplace deep within you, whisper, "Now is the time. Today is the day."

How, you wonder, does one get saved? Simple. Acknowledge. Ask. Accept.

Acknowledge your sin. Confess it to God. (Romans 3:23; Isaiah 53:6)
Ask God to forgive you. Call on Him. (John 3:16; 1 John 1:9)
Accept His forgiveness. Consent to His Lordship. (John 1:12; Romans 10:9–10)
Abound in your faith. Cultivate it daily. (Colossians 2:6–7; 2 Peter 3:18)

Welcome to the family!

Be blessed!
Michele

ABOUT THE AUTHOR

MICHELE HUEY is an award-winning author whose published books include several novels, as well as compilations from her award-winning newspaper column. Her favorite setting for her fiction is western Pennsylvania, where she lives with her husband, Dean, who provides her with much fodder for her writing. The mother of three grown children and the grandmother of nine, she loves hiking, camping, swimming, and reading, and is an avid (and sometimes rabid) Pittsburgh Pirates fan. Visit Michele online at michelehuey.com.

BOOKS BY MICHELE HUEY

FICTION

The Heart Remembers
Mid-LOVE Crisis (formerly *Before I Die*)
Getaway Mountain: PennWoods Mystery Book 1
Ghost Mountain: PennWoods Mystery Book 2

DEVOTIONAL

Minute Meditations: Meeting God in Everyday Experiences
I Lift Up My Eyes: Minute Meditations Vol. 2
God, Me, & a Cup of Tea
God, Me & a Cup of Tea for the Seasons
God, Me, & a Cup of Tea, Volume 3

Look for these titles on Amazon in Kindle and paperback formats.

CONTACT INFORMATION

Email: michelehueybooks@gmail.com

Website: michelehuey. com

Blog: godmetea. com

You'll also find me on Goodreads, Facebook, Twitter, Google Plus, LinkedIn, Instagram, and Pinterest. Connect with me!

Dear Reader,

I hope you enjoyed this third volume of *God, Me & a Cup of Tea.* Please consider submitting a review and/or rating on Amazon and Goodreads (goodreads.com/michelehuey). Your feedback is greatly appreciated.

Blessings,
Michele

Made in the USA
Columbia, SC
10 April 2024

34187464R00196